MW01671074

Little Fingers

Creative Ideas for the Young at Art

Sandy Cosgrove
Carol Wellein

DALE SEYMOUR PUBLICATIONS

Cover design: Rachel Gage

Copyright © 1987 by Dale Seymour Publications. All rights reserved. No part of this publication may be reproduced in any form or by any means without the prior written permission of the publisher.

Printed in the United States of America. Published simultaneously in Canada.

Order number DS11709
ISBN 0-86651-362-0

DALE
SEYMOUR
PUBLICATIONS
P.O. BOX 10888
PALO ALTO, CA 94303

3 4 5 6 7 8 9 10 11 12-MA-95 94 93 92 91

CONTENTS

INTRODUCTION

Art is not just a period set aside for making things. It is a time to explore, experiment, create, and discover. It should be an exciting time for the child and the teacher, a time that enriches the classroom experience and brings feelings of joy and accomplishment.

This book provides a series of art ideas—both open-ended and project-oriented. There should be room for both in the art curriculum, thus creating a balance between creative expression and developmental use of skills. Many of these activities can easily be integrated into the total curriculum. We hope you will feel free to "adapt" these ideas to your unique classroom and the availability of materials.

Little Fingers is for the busy educator seeking supplemental help for art instruction. The "child-tested" activities are for children three to eight years old. Simple, easy-to-follow directions, motivational techniques, and art concepts are combined to encourage creativity and experimentation with line, shape, color, and texture. Original poems and songs are also provided to correlate with the lessons. A variety of media are utilized to maintain interest. Throughout the book are helpful tips for fostering adult/child relationships through art.

Ideas are arranged in monthly sequence. Seasonal and holiday lessons are included in the appropriate month followed by a series of specific developmental skills and concepts that can be used at any time. It is suggested that the teacher read and prepare in advance for each lesson.

We hope *Little Fingers* will encourage you to try new ideas, stimulate your creativity, and inspire you to look at the world around you in a whole new way.

Sandy Cosgrove
Carol Wellein

How to Stock Your Art Closet

Collect the following items at the beginning of the school year to supplement the basic supplies provided by your school:

- A large box of paper scraps
- scraps of fabrics and felt
- buttons, beads, shells
- yarn in assorted colors
- wooden craft sticks
- cotton swabs
- cotton balls
- assorted sponges
- dried beans and peas
- pipe cleaners
- variety of cardboard boxes
- cardboard—sheets, corrugated
- jars, cans (coffee, juice, etc.)
- paper lunch bags
- magazines, catalogs
- wallpaper sample books
- bottle caps
- paper plates
- paper tubes
- paper doilies
- spools in assorted sizes
- clothespins
- straws
- string
- glitter

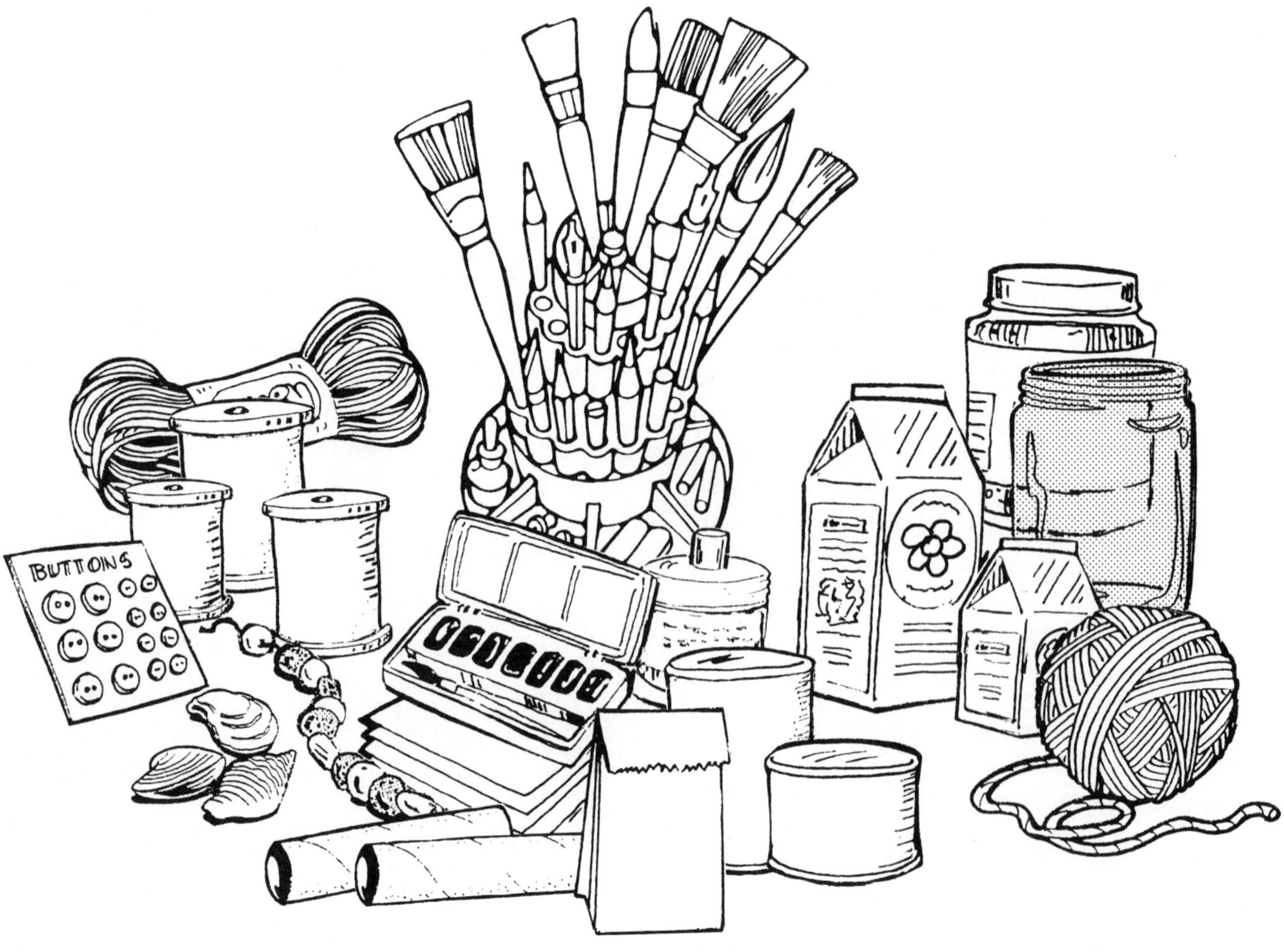

Learning about Color

Color is all around us. Colors can show emotion, can be warm or cool, can be mixed to form new colors, can be identified, and can be applied in a variety of ways.

The following activities can be used singly or in combination for the teaching of color:

- Find two pictures, one containing mostly warm colors (red, yellow, and orange) and one containing mostly cool colors (blue, green, and purple). Discuss how each picture makes you feel, identifying the color differences. Have class make their own crayon pictures using all warm or all cool colors.

- Using vegetable dye, show how to mix two colors to make a new color. Fold paper towel and dip edges into two primary colors. See how they mix to form a new (secondary) color.

- Identify colors according to the seasons and holidays (orange for Halloween, green for March,etc.).

- To sharpen visual discrimination skills, make color-patterned necklaces by threading beads in color combinations such as: yellow/blue, yellow/blue, yellow/blue.

- Tear a variety of colored paper leaves and glue to the trunk of a tree for a fall picture (or use watercolors for leaves instead).

- Place bowls of butter icing on work tables. Let children add drops of two vegetable dyes to make a new color for the icing. Spread on oatmeal cookies for snack time.

Motivation: Read one or all of the following books, *Orange Is a Color* by Sharon Lerner, *Little Blue and Little Yellow* by Leo Lionni, *The Great Blueness and Other Predicaments* by Arnold Lobel. Use any of the musical activities suggested on the record "Color Me A Rainbow" produced by Sharron Lucky for Melody House.

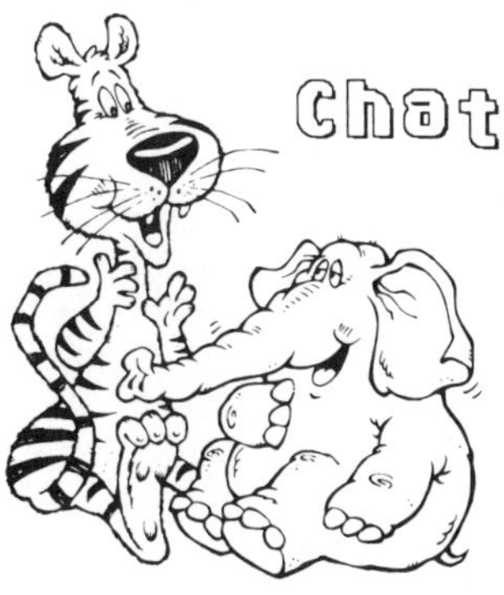

Chatter Box

It is important to use appropriate art vocabulary wherever possible. Familiarity with these terms builds understanding as the child develops. Also, vocabulary that indicates direction (top, middle, center, etc.) is rapidly added to the children's comprehension as they engage in art activities.

SEPTEMBER IDEAS

Can You Find the Color?

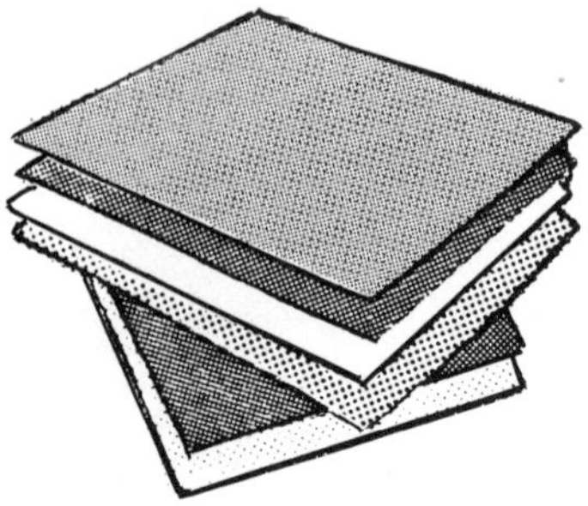

Materials
- colored paper
- old magazines
- glue
- white shelf paper

Activity

Hold up pieces of colored paper one at a time, and ask the children where they see that color. Have them stand by that color in the room. When they can identify the color, they may be seated. (Also, they may find these colors on themselves and repeat above process.)

Directions

Hand each child a piece of colored paper. Ask all those who have orange (green, red, etc.) to stand. Have them sit again as you name their colors. Give each child a magazine or old catalog. Ask them to tear out the color(s) you name. Have each paste his example on a long sheet of white shelf paper that will become a color banner. Hang these around the room. A different color can be introduced each day.

Extension

Use crayons in the colors(s) you have introduced on drawing paper. Older children could sponge paint with learned colors.

Leaf Rubbings

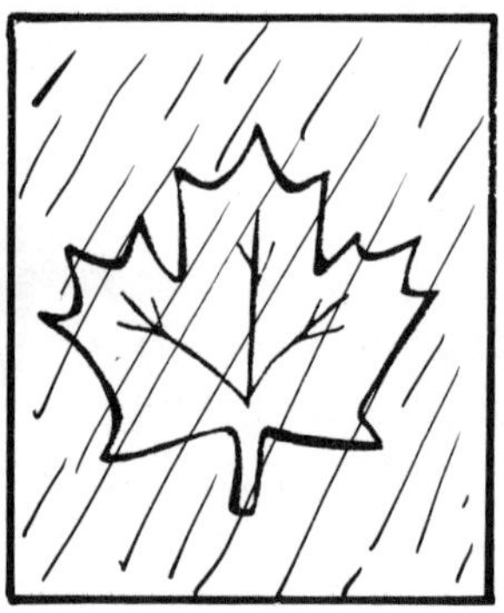

Materials
- good-sized leaves
- crayons (with paper removed)
- newsprint
- masking tape

Directions

On one of your walks outside, have each child find one fairly large leaf. (Older children may use several.) Place leaf/leaves on table. Secure with masking tape rolled underneath leaf so it will not move. Place a sheet of newsprint over the top and use side of peeled crayons to rub (pressing fairly hard) leaf pattern onto sheet of paper. When several leaves are used, choose colors in shades of red, orange, yellow, and brown.

Flower Matching Game

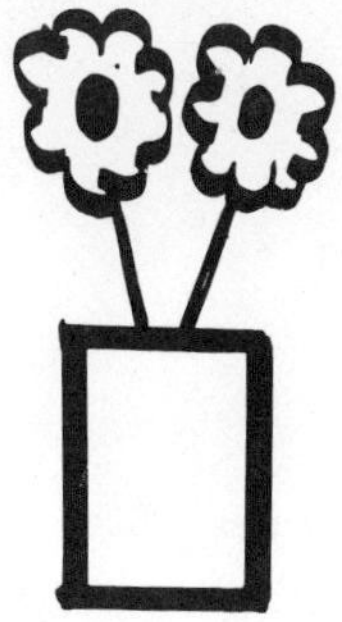

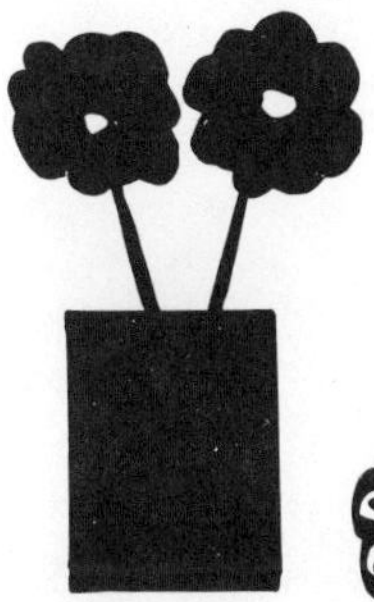

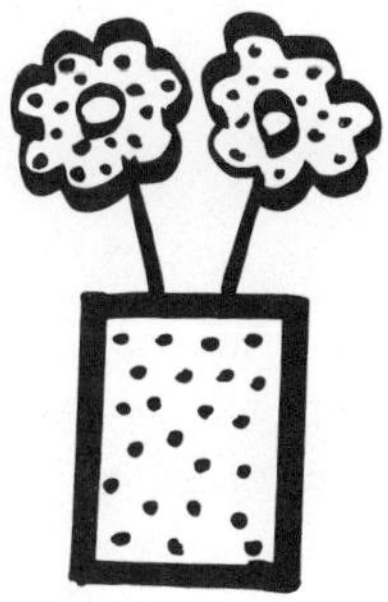

Concept

Colors can be identified by matching.The following game teaches color identification, but it also incorporates counting and reading readiness skills through matching and counting. The materials for this game should be prepared in advance by the teacher.

Preparation

Cover a juice can with construction paper for each color that is to be introduced, using at least three different colors. Cut out simple flower shapes from the same colors used on cans. Glue or tape these shapes to pipe cleaner stems.

Game Directions

1. Give one flower to each child.
2. Ask each child to place his/her flower in the vase that matches the color of his/her flower.
3. As the children become more familiar with colors, increase the number and variety of colored flowers.
4. Ask them to count the number of flowers they have before putting them in the appropriate vases.
5. Have the class help count the total number of flowers in each vase.

Motivation: Use the song "GettingTo Know You" from *The King and I* as motivation for the next two activities.

Shoe Portrait

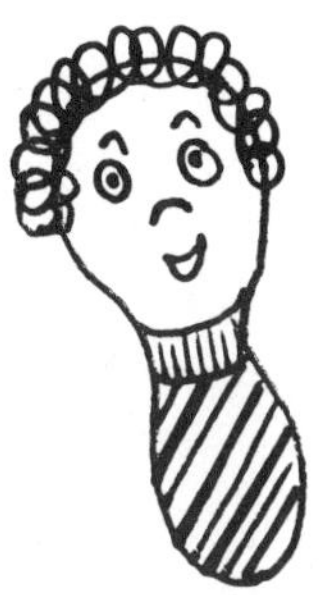

Concept

A creative activity can be used to express knowledge of oneself. (Talk about how each of us looks. Discuss types and colors of hair and eyes, and shapes of noses and mouths. Try the activity in front of a mirror. Go on to discuss our clothing—colors, stripes, etc.)

Materials

- 9" x 12" drawing paper
- pencil, scissors
- crayons or markers

Directions

Have each child trace a classmate's foot (with shoe on) onto drawing paper. Cut out shoe shapes. Add faces and clothing with crayons or markers. This makes a great "Getting To Know You" bulletin board.

Personality Puppet

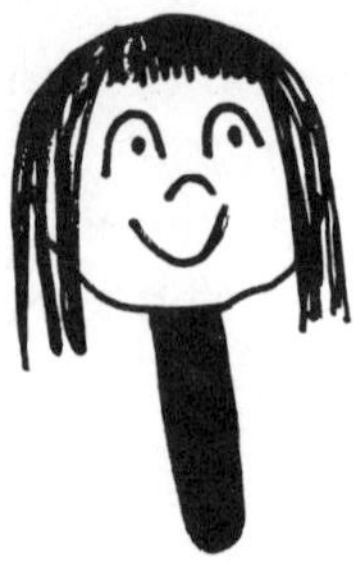

Materials

- wooden craft stick
- construction paper circle—3" diameter
- glue
- crumbled tissue or yarn (for hair)
- crayons or markers

Directions

Draw a face on the paper circle. Add hair and glue the face at the top of the craft stick.

Torn-Paper Apple Trees

Motivation: Read the following poem (using hand motions) to the class before beginning this activity.

Three Little Apples

Three little apples sitting in a tree
Looking as happy as they could be
I pulled those apples—one, two, three
And I made a juicy treat for me

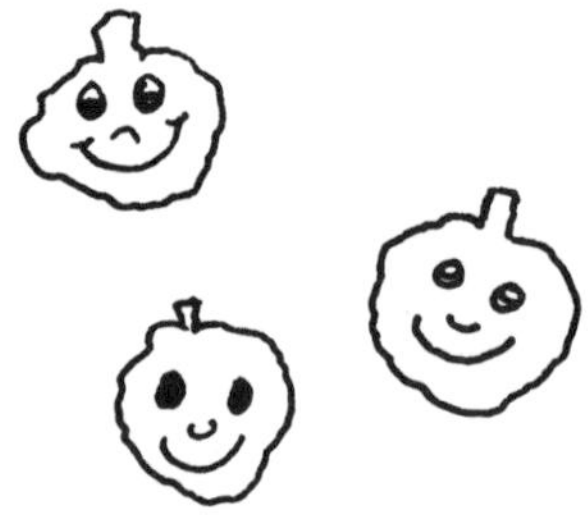

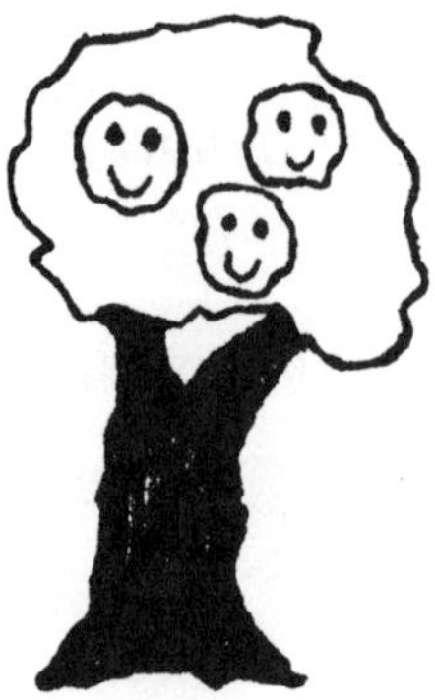

Materials

- small copies of poem above
- 6" x 9" sheet drawing paper
- construction paper: 6" x 41/2" brown, 6" x 41/2" green, scraps of red for apples
- glue
- black crayon

Directions

Tell the children that scissors cannot be used. Then have each child tear a trunk shape from the brown construction paper. Glue to white background paper. Using the green construction paper, tear a round shape for leaves.

Hint

For a good circle, start tearing just corners so your shape will not be too small. Glue this on top of trunk. Tear three small red apples and glue on tree. With black crayon, draw smiling faces on apples. Attach poem copy to finished tree.

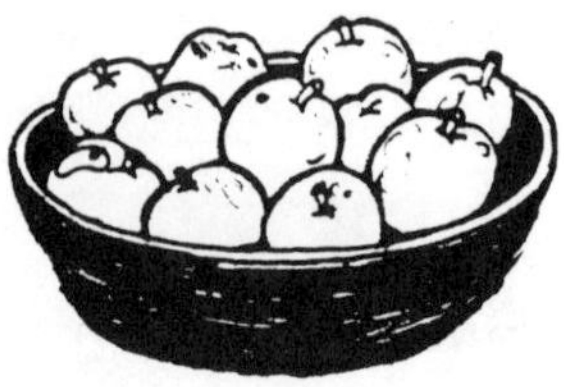

Extension

Fix some kind of apple treat for snack time.

Giant Fingerpaint Popsicle

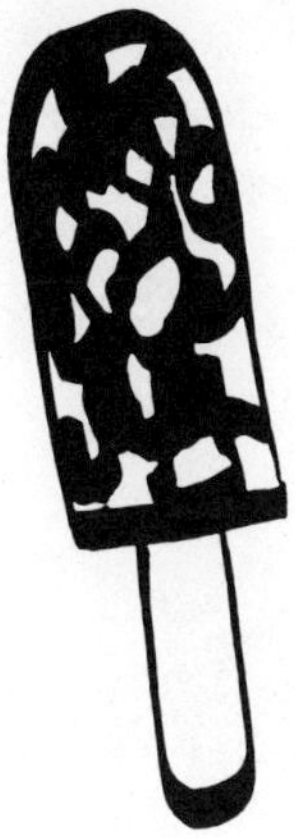

Concept

Two colors can be mixed to make a new color.

Materials

- red and yellow fingerpaint
- fingerpaint paper
- water, sponge
- scissors, glue
- paint stirrer or brown construction paper (cut to resemble an ice cream stick)

Directions

Day one —Place one dab of yellow and one of red on wet fingerpaint paper. Mix these colors together with both hands. Discover how red and yellow have made orange. Let dry.

Day two — Cut a giant "popsicle" shape from orange fingerpainting. Glue paint stirrer or large brown paper stick to back of your "Giant Popsicle."

Clean-up Procedure

1. Place several sheets of newspaper on floor.
2. Fill two buckets with water and place on newspaper.
3. Beside the buckets, provide a stack of paper towels and a trash can.
4. After fingerpainting, children proceed down this clean-up assembly line.

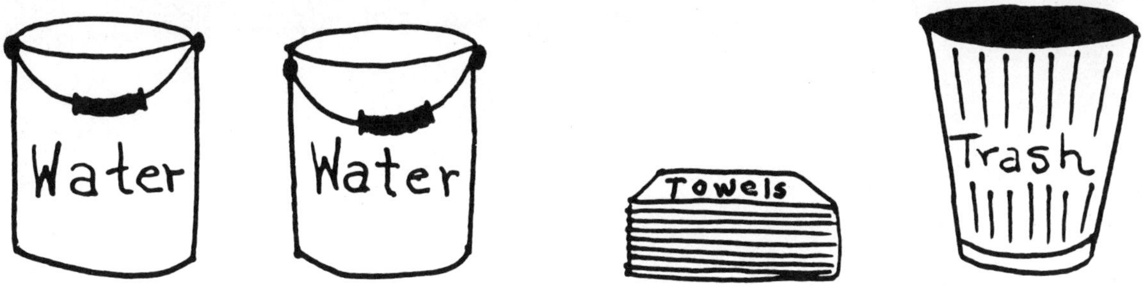

Extension

Make frozen snacks by filling ice cube trays with cherry and lemon drink prepared from powdered mix. Let children help mix so that they can see the color change. Freeze and serve on *day two.*

Tissue See-Through

Concept

Colors may be overlapped to form new colors.

Motivation: Hold up waxed paper. Hold up tissue. Discuss how both are *transparent.* Compare them to a piece of construction paper, which is *opaque.* Using these two terms, name other objects that are either *transparent* or *opaque.*

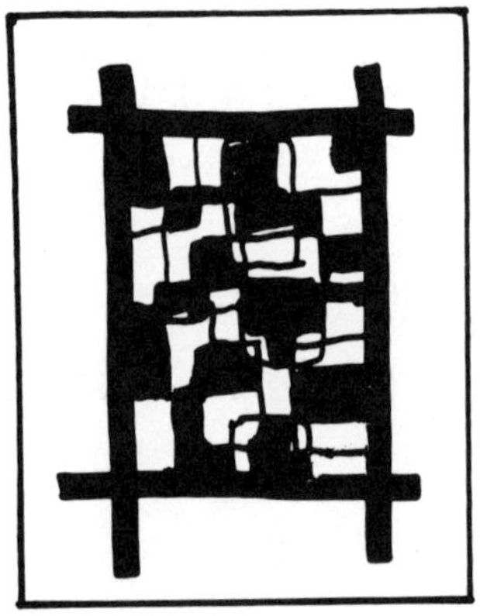

Materials

- vegetable oil
- cotton balls
- waxed paper—2 pieces per child
- yellow and blue tissue (approximately 2" x 2")
- construction paper strips
- glue

Directions

Use cotton ball to coat one whole piece of waxed paper with oil. Lay tissue on oiled paper, overlapping colors to form new color (green). Oil second piece of waxed paper and place on top. The oil makes the tissue translucent. Frame your see-through design with paper strips. Mount on window so the light will shine through.

Scissors Skills

Early in the year, it is a good idea to introduce scissors and cutting skills to younger children. We recommend that this be taught to your four-, five-, and six-year olds now. January is a better time for introducing this skill to three-year-olds.

To motivate discussion, we suggest using two posters. One should show the materials that can be cut with scissors such as actual scraps of yarn, string, paper, cloth, foil, cardboard, styrofoam, and plastic. The second poster should show things that cannot and should not be cut. Using pictures cut from magazines you could include examples such as hair, pets, toys, stuffed animals, and objects too hard to cut (metal, wood, glass, etc.).

Next, give each child a pair of scissors. Instruct him/her to place the thumb in the top hole and one or two fingers in the bottom hole. Pretend the scissors are big fish. Open the fish's mouth wide and close it. Practice this several times so that the child begins to feel the rhythm of the open-close motion.

Basic Safety Rules:

1. Never point or poke scissors at anyone.
2. Keep scissors closed when not in use.
3. Always carry them closed, in a point-down position with hand closed tightly around blades.

Scissors Storage Suggestion:

Inverted egg cartons with a hole punched in each dome provide a safe and convenient storage place for classroom scissors.

Cutting Collage

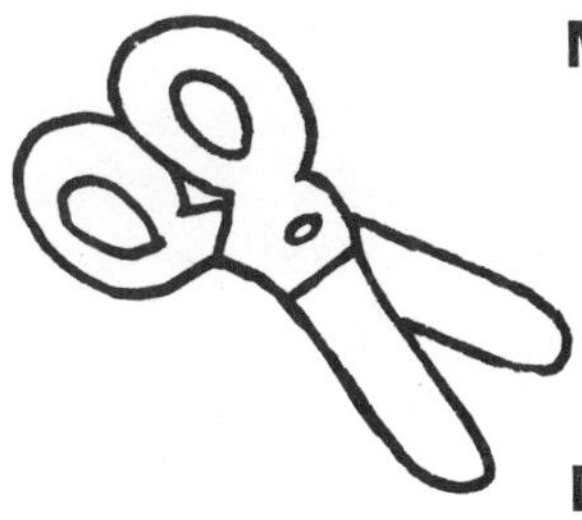

Materials

- all kinds of scrap yarn, paper, string, foil, styrofoam, plastic, straws, fabric, cardboard, etc.
- construction paper —1 piece per child
- glue

Directions

Have each child practice cutting the various materials. Then glue down on background paper to make the collage.

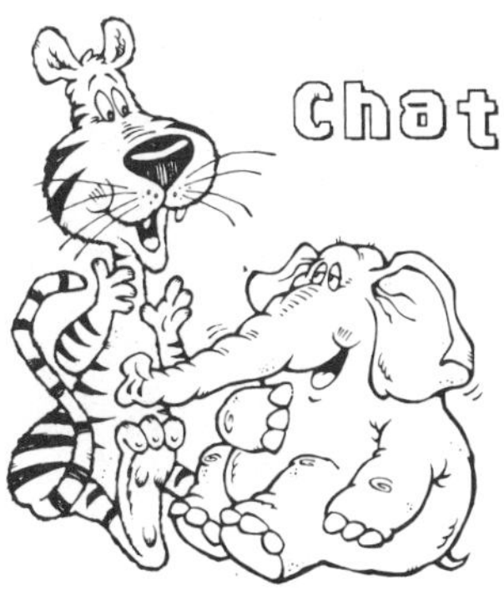

Chatter Box

Children should be given the feeling that whatever they create is appreciated. They will be able to express themselves creatively when in a warm, friendly atmosphere where they are appreciated for themselves. This means that each child's work will not be compared to another child's work or criticized because it doesn't suit the "tastes" of others.

OCTOBER IDEAS

Autumn Leaves

Motivation: The song below may be used as motivation and/or follow-up for the following project. (Sung to tune of "London Bridge Is Falling Down")

Autumn Leaves

Autumn leaves are falling down,
falling down, falling down,
Autumn leaves are falling down,
Red, orange, yellow, and brown.

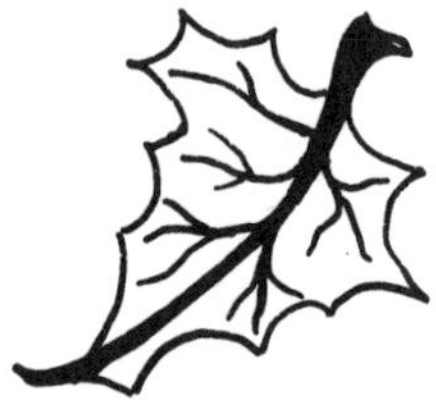

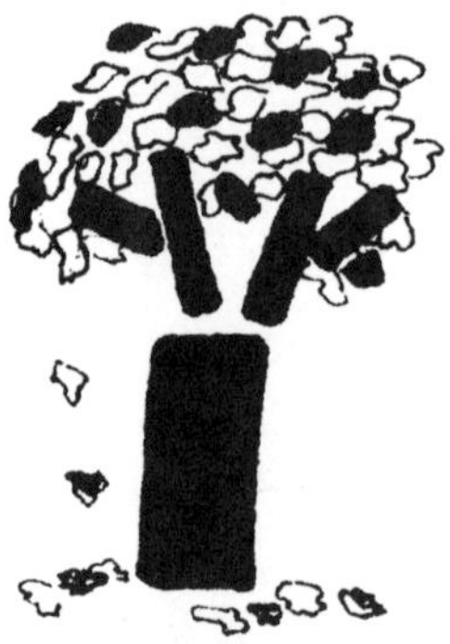

Materials

- 9" x 12" construction paper for background
- various-sized precut strips of brown corrugated cardboard for branches
- 1 1/2" x 4 1/2" corrugated cardboard for trunk
- scraps of red, yellow, orange and brown construction paper
- glue

Directions

Glue cardboard strips on background paper to resemble a tree with branches. Tear scraps of colored construction paper into small pieces for leaves. Glue these on branches, ground, and in the air.

Painted Leaves

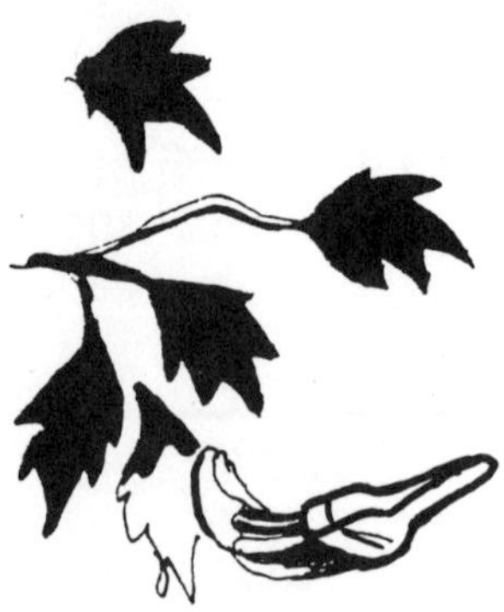

Materials (for younger children)

- precut white leaf shapes
- small squares (approximately 2" x 2") of tissue in fall colors
- small bowls of water

Directions

Slightly crumple tissue, dip in water, and rub on leaf. The color of the tissue will appear as you rub. Use a variety of colors to cover leaf completely.

Materials (for older children)

- leaf patterns
- 9" x 12" white drawing paper
- pencils
- scissors
- watercolors, brushes, water

Directions

Thoroughly wet white paper. Experiment by applying several colors, and watch these colors as they blend. Let dry. Trace leaf patterns on painting and cut out. A watercolor wash causes paper to curl, so it is best to paint first and cut second.

Motivation: This poem may be used to introduce the following Halloween projects.

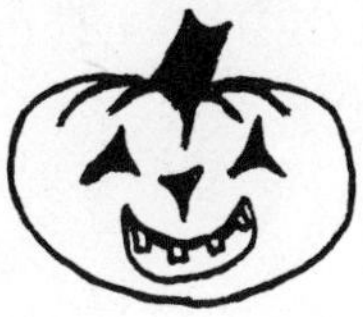
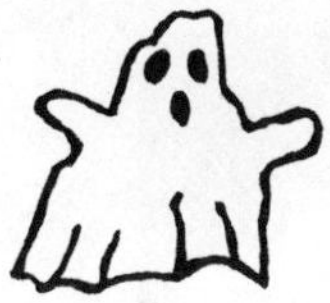

Halloween Fun

Halloween is coming soon
It's time for lots of fun.
We'll see a witch fly near the moon
A ghost is on the run
Jack o'lantern smiles are seen
These things we'll make for Halloween.

Torn-Paper Witch

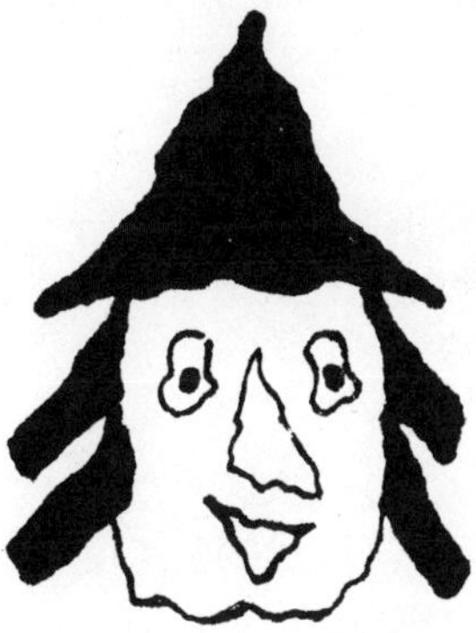

Materials

- 9" x 12" green or yellow construction paper for background
- 6" x 5 1/2" orange construction paper
- 6" x 5 1/2" black construction paper
- glue

Directions

Tear a circle shape from orange paper for head. Tear a triangle shape from black paper for hat. (Tear small amounts and tear slowly.) Strips torn from triangle may be used for hair and face. Glue head and then hat to background paper. From black scraps, tear hair, eyes, nose, and mouth and glue to head.

Flying Ghosts

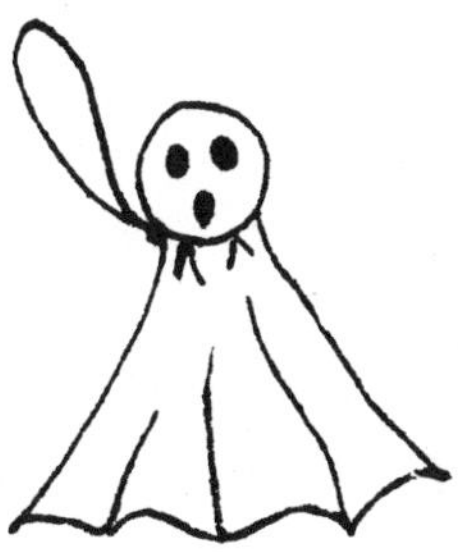

Materials

- facial tissue or 10" x 10" piece of white cloth
- 1 cotton ball
- string
- black marking pen

Directions

Have each child place cotton ball in center of tissue or cloth. Gather material around cotton ball and tie with a string, leaving long ends on the string. Draw in a face with the marking pen. Hang flying ghosts around the room.

Ghost Stencils

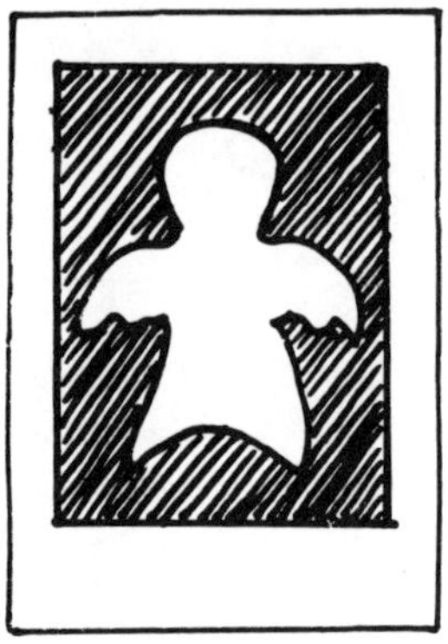

Materials

- Ghost stencils precut from piece of 9" x 12" cardboard
- white tempera paint
- sponges for printing
- 9" x 12" black construction paper
- black markers

Directions

Place stencil on top of black construction paper. Using an "up-down" motion with sponge, fill in the ghost shape with white tempera. Let dry. Add eyes and mouth with marker, if desired.

Tissue Ghosts

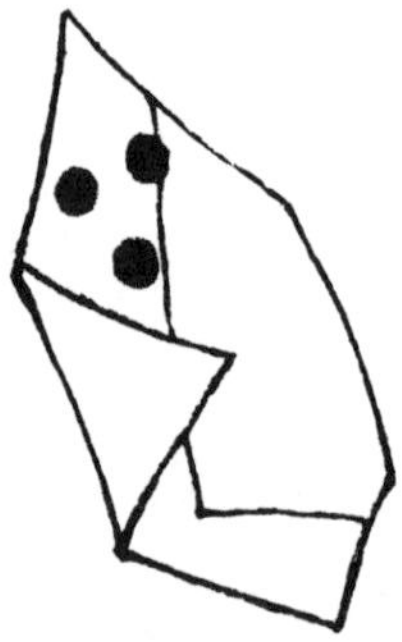

Materials

- 1 white facial tissue
- 9" x 12" black construction paper for background
- paper scraps (for facial features)
- glue

Directions

Have each child open a tissue and fold edges into a triangle-shape. Glue to black paper. Add face.

Triangle Witch

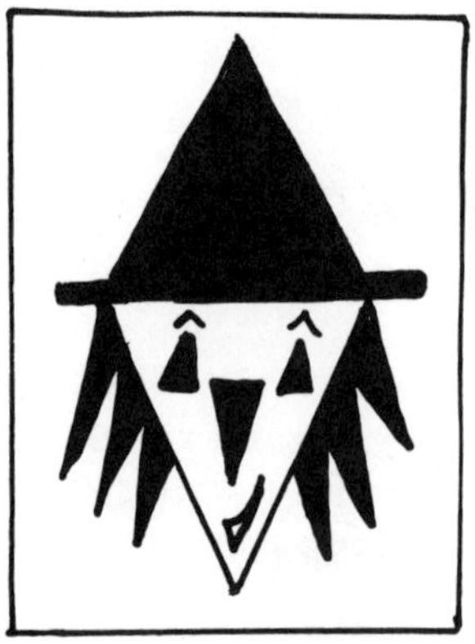

Concept

One shape can be repeated to form a recognizable object.

Materials

- 9" x 12" orange and black construction paper
- black construction paper scraps
- glue, scissors

Directions

Fold orange and black paper in half. Cut a triangle shape on the fold from each color. Glue black triangle for hat at the top of the orange triangle (face). Cut a black paper strip for brim of hat, and glue. Add facial features and hair from scraps or use black markers.

Hint

Patterns or precut triangle shapes may be used for younger children.

Motivation: Use the following song and its motions for the art project below: (Sung to the tune of "Did You Ever See a Lassie?". Additional verses can be sung for the "old witch" and "white ghost.")

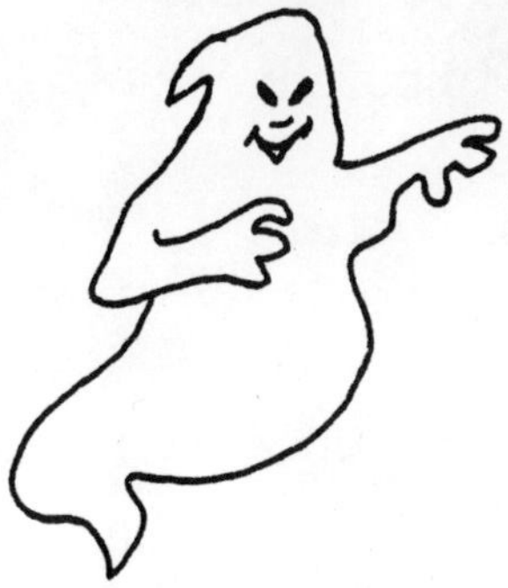

Did You Ever See a Black Cat?
Did you ever see a black cat, a black cat, a black cat
Did you ever see a black cat on Halloween Night
Go this way and that way
(*use your own motions*)
Go this way and that way
Did you ever see a black cat go this way and that?

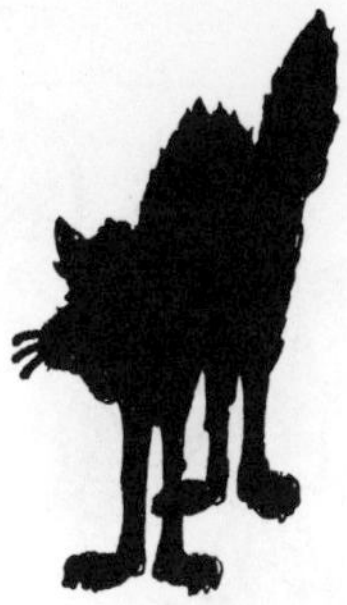

Torn-Paper Cat

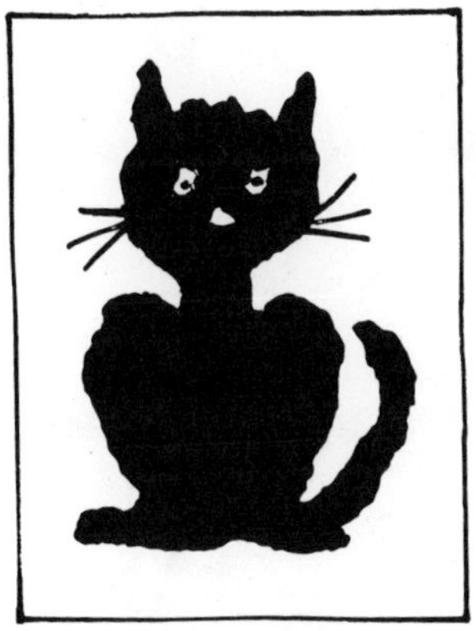

Concept

Paper can be torn to form a recognizable object.

Materials

- 9" x 12" construction paper for background
- 9" x 12" black construction paper
- orange and yellow construction paper scraps
- glue

Directions

Tear a round shape from the black paper for a head. From the same piece of paper, tear a larger oval for body, a tail, and two small triangle-shaped ears. Glue to background paper. Tear two yellow eyes and an orange nose and whiskers. Glue to head for face.

3-D Bag Pumpkins

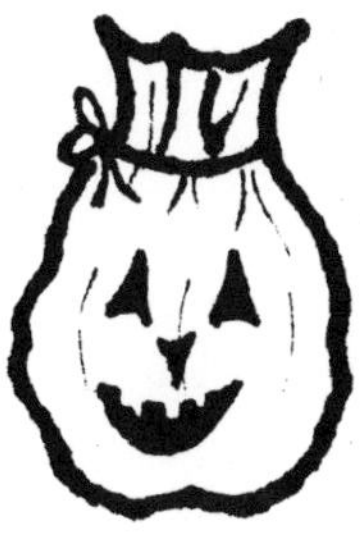

Materials

- any size paper bag
- orange tempera, brushes
- newspaper (for stuffing)
- string or yarn (green or orange)
- green crepe paper or green tempera for stem

Directions

Stuff bag with newspaper. Gather bag together at top and tie with string or yarn. Paint pumpkin with orange tempera. The stem may be painted green or wrapped with green crepe paper. Let dry. (If desired, features can be cut from black paper.)

Pumpkin Patch

October Bulletin Board Idea

Materials

- brown wrapping paper (enough to cover a bulletin board or to hang as a large mural)
- green and orange tempera paints
- brushes, black marker

Directions

Teacher should mount brown paper and paint a trailing green vine with leaves across the paper. During the month of October, have each child paint a pumpkin in the patch. After the pumpkin dries, add child's name with black marker.

Silly Pumpkins

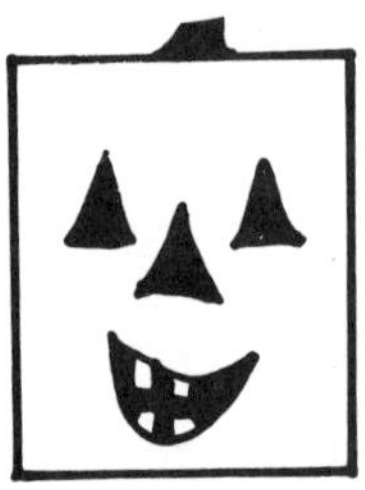

Concept

Shapes can be recognized and named.

Materials

- 9" x 12" orange construction paper
- green and black construction paper scraps
- precut circle, square, rectangle, and triangle cardboard
- patterns (sized to fit 9" x 12" paper)
- pencils, glue, and scissors

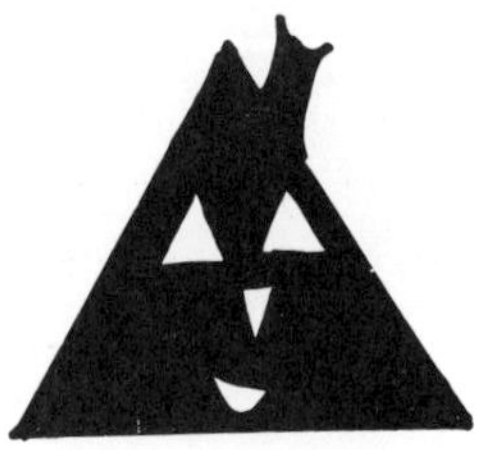

Directions

Discuss shapes with class. Find examples of shapes around the room. Ask what shape a pumpkin usually is, and talk about what fun it would be to see a "different" shaped pumpkin. Have each child choose a shape, trace onto orange paper, and cut out. Faces and stems can be cut out from paper scraps and added to the pumpkin.

Walnut Ships (In observance of Columbus Day)

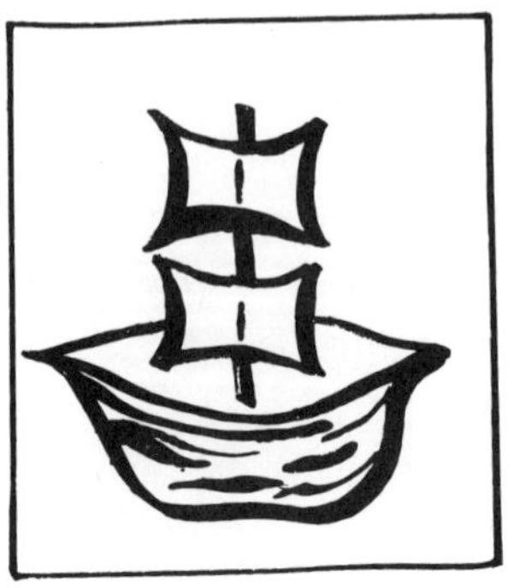

Materials

- 1/2 walnut shell (per child)
- white paper scraps
- clay, playdough or salt dough
- toothpicks, scissors

Directions

Fill walnut shell with clay. Cut two small sails out of paper scraps. Push toothpick through each sail and set in clay.

Teaching Shape Identification

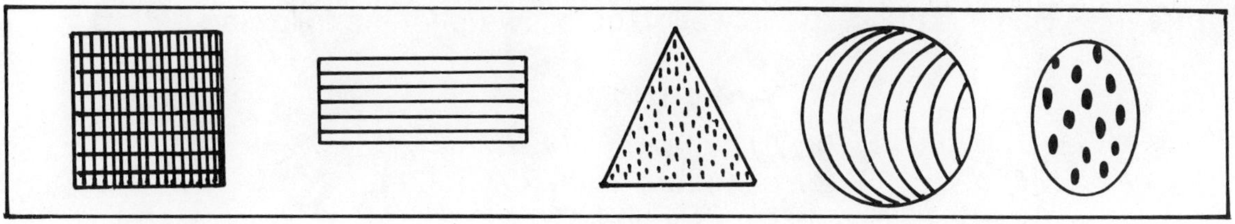

Identifying Shapes

Shapes can be named and identified. Shapes can be taught by using the usual precut patterns or by pointing out objects in nature and in the classroom. These are the five basic shapes to be mastered at the early childhood level: *square, rectangle, triangle, circle* and *oval.* Many of the November activities are structured around the study of shape.

Teaching Shape Identification

- Verbal and Cognitive Recognition
  a. Give each child a large precut shape. Hold up a shape. Those children with the matching shape are to hold up their shape, calling out its name as you go along.
  b. Put all five shapes on the flannel board. Cover the board. Remove one shape. Ask the class to identify the missing shape.

- Give each child a plastic sandwich bag. Take the class outside and find objects of different shapes on the ground. Put the objects in the bags. Bring inside and glue to cardboard.

- Have each one choose their favorite shape, name it, trace it, and color it. Teacher can then write "This is (Billy's) triangle."

- Glue colored, precut shapes onto black paper to make a picture or design.

- Have several children form a basic shape by using their bodies. Ask the other children to identify the shape made by the group.

- As children leave, hand each one a shape. Ask them to find a matching object at home that they can bring in the next day.

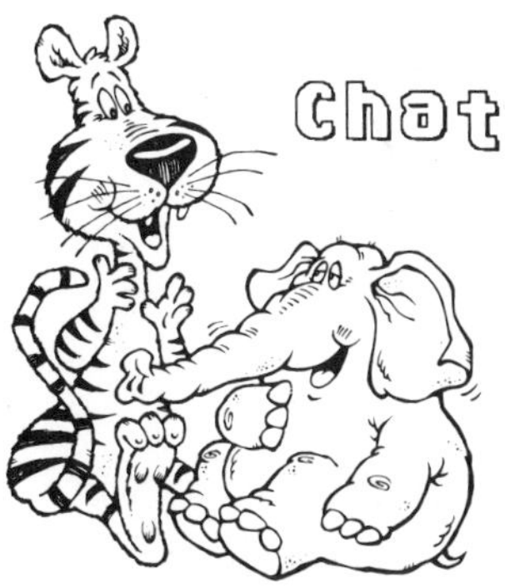

Chatter Box

The final product is not the most important aspect of the art experience for young children. Rather, it is the time they are given to explore, experiment, and discover the possibilities and limitations of various materials and procedures. Projects are fine, but it is in the "doing" that the most learning and enjoyment are found.

NOVEMBER IDEAS

Motivation: Use this poem as motivation or follow-up for the following project.

Perky Turkey
Perky Turkey likes to say
Gobble, gobble all the day.
His feathers wiggle to and fro.
His bright red wattle seems to glow.
He struts around with head held high
Trying so hard to reach the sky.

Perky Turkey

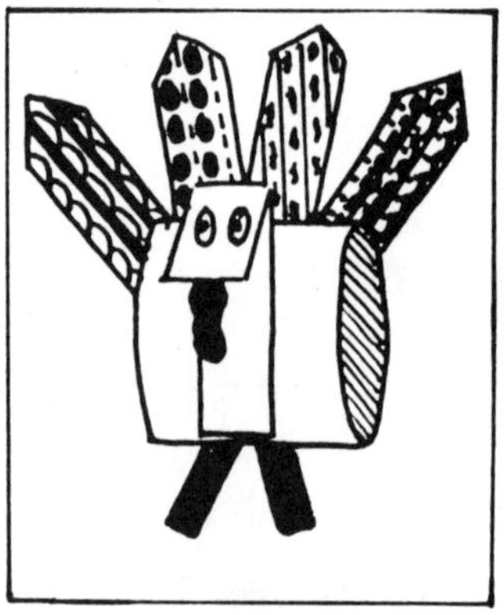

Concept

A rectangle can be formed into a three-dimensional shape.

Materials

- 9" x 12" construction paper for background
- 4" x 9" brown construction paper
- 2" x 6" brown construction paper
- wallpaper strips (from sample books)
- yellow and red construction paper scraps
- scissors, glue
- pencil

Directions

Trace around fingers (not thumb) on background paper. Glue four wallpaper feathers on top of each finger. Form a cylinder with the large rectangle and glue at base of feathers. Fold down smaller brown rectangle 11/2" from top and glue to cylinder to form head. Add red wattle, eyes, and feet.

Egg Carton Turkey

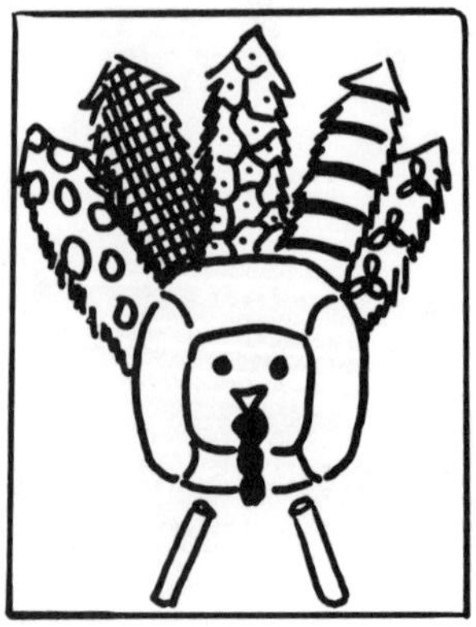

Concept

Shapes can be combined to form new shapes.

Materials

- half of 9" x 12" piece of construction paper
- egg carton section
- wallpaper samples, paper scraps
- straws
- glue, scissors

Directions

Cut five feathers, each about 4" long, from wallpaper samples. Take one cup section from egg carton, invert it, and glue on top of feathers. Add straw legs, red wattle, orange beak, and black eyes.

Simple Turkey Puppet

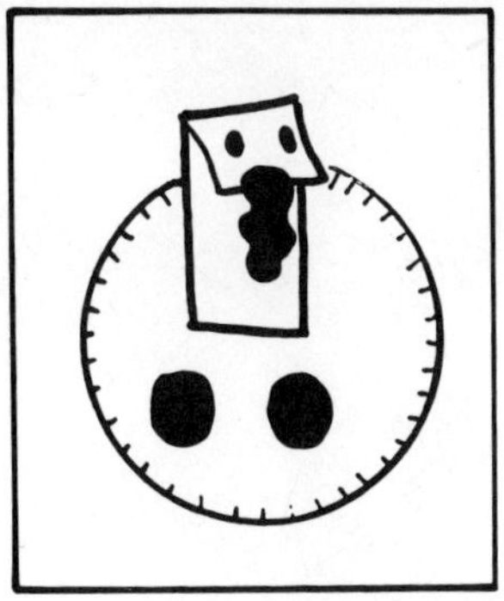

Concept

Three-dimensional shapes can be used to represent animals.

Materials

- 6" paper plate (dessert-size)
- tempera paints—red and yellow
- sponges
- 6" x 1 1/2" brown paper strips
- red and black scraps of construction paper
- glue, scissors

Directions

Day one —Sponge paint paper plates.
Day two —Cut two small holes for fingers in paper plate. Glue on brown strip at top and fold down about 11/2" to form head and neck. Add red wattle, beak, and black eyes. Have children insert fingers in holes to form turkeys' legs.

Salt Dough Indian Necklace

Concept

Shapes can be formed by molding.

Ingredients

- 1 cup salt
- 1/2 cup cornstarch
- 1/2 cup boiling water
- food coloring (1 color per batch)

Mix all ingredients together and cook until thick.
Place dough in a plastic bag to keep moist until used.

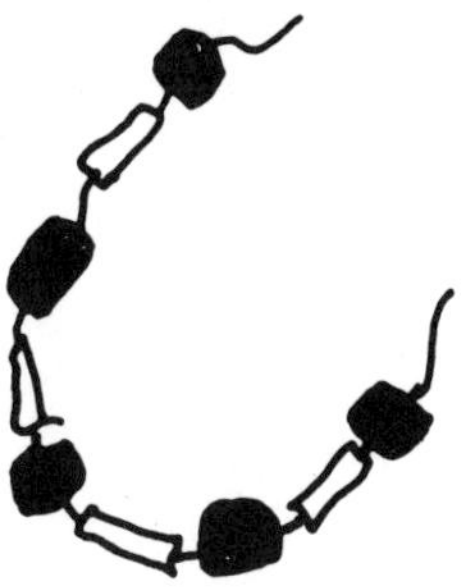

Materials

- yarn or string
- toothpicks
- uncooked pasta

Directions

Warn children that this dough tastes terrible. Shape the dough into beads and push toothpick through each. Stick finished beads in modeling clay to dry. Make several different-colored beads. When beads are thoroughly dry, string on yarn alternately with macaroni. (Make sure holes in beads are large enough for yarn. Masking tape can be wrapped on end of yarn for easy stringing.)

Indian Teepees

Motivation: Discuss one kind of Indian dwelling used by the Plains tribes known as the "teepee." What shape does it appear to have? What shapes are used for decoration of the teepee?

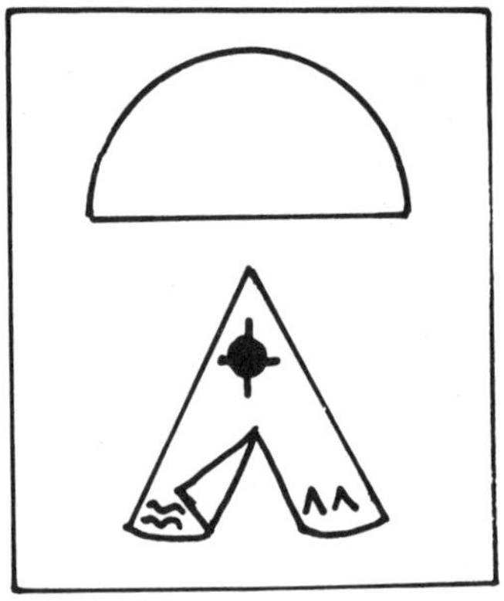

Concept (for older children)

A half-circle can form a cone shape.

Materials

- 9" x 12" construction paper
- crayons
- stapler
- scissors

Directions

Cut out a large circle drawn on 9" x 12" paper. Cut this circle in half. Each child gets one semicircle. Decorate with crayons, keeping the rounded edge facing the child. Pull points together to form cone shape and staple. Cut slit and fold back for door.

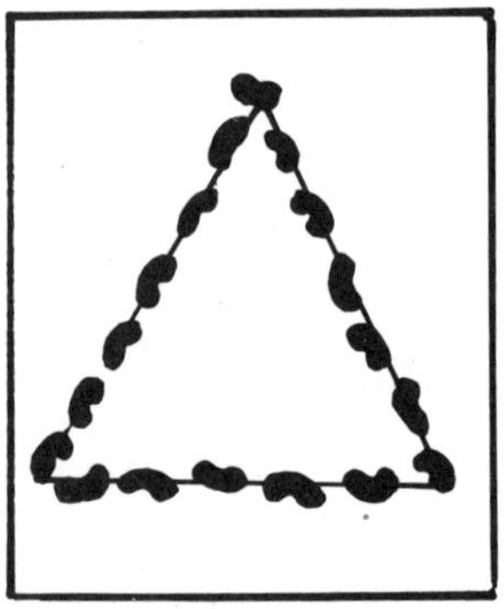

Concept (for younger children)

A teepee can be made from a triangle.

Materials

- manila paper
- large triangle pattern
- marking pen
- lima beans
- glue

Directions

Teacher should draw triangle on manila paper for each child. Have child put small dots of glue along the black line. Add lima beans on glue.

Indian Rhythm

Motivation: The following poem may be used as motivation and follow-up for the next two projects.The teacher should clap out the basic beat where accent marks appear, while children use their instruments. Discuss what kinds of instruments Indians used.

Háppy Índian bráves are wé (4 beats)
Hópping and skípping in tíme (3 beats)
Béat our tóm-toms óne, twó, thrée (4 beats)
Sháke our ráttles so fíne. (3 beats)

Indian Seed Rattle

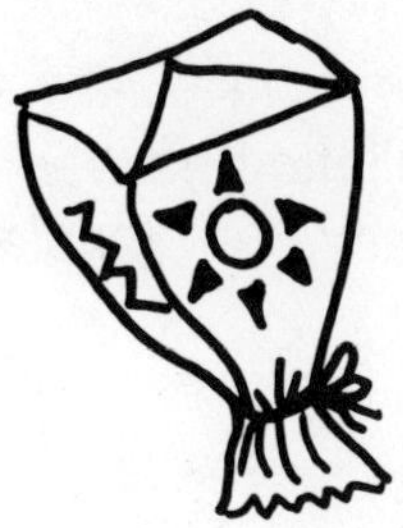

Materials
- brown paper lunch bags
- yarn or string
- felt markers, crayons, or tempera paints
- seeds and/or dried beans

Directions
Decorate bags with Indian symbols or designs.
Place a handful of beans or seeds in each bag. Twist and tie end of bag with yarn.

Tom-Tom

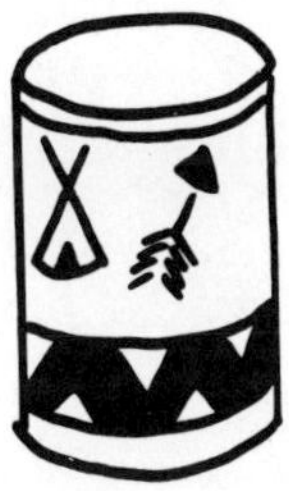

Materials
- 1-pound coffee cans or oatmeal boxes with lids
- paper to cover
- glue
- felt markers or crayons

Directions
Decorate paper precut to fit container.Cover container with lid.

Indian Sand Painting

Concept
Shapes can be drawn on a textured surface.

Materials
- sandpaper
- crayons

Directions
Have each child choose an Indian design or symbol to draw on the sandpaper with crayons.

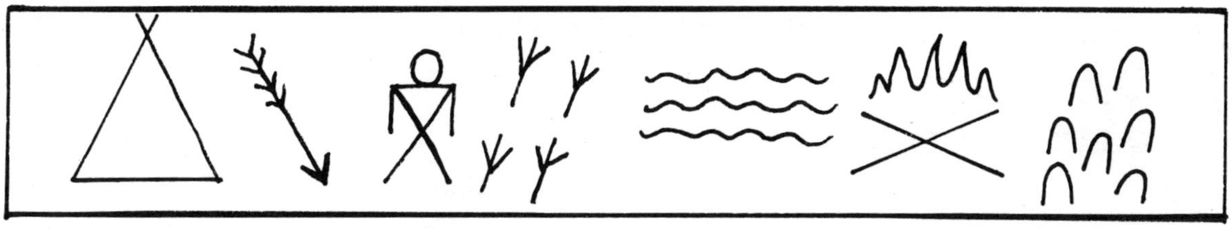

Horn of Plenty

November Bulletin Board Idea

Motivation: Discuss autumn as a time of harvest and of plenty. The bulletin board should celebrate our "land of plenty" using the symbol of the horn of plenty/cornucopia.

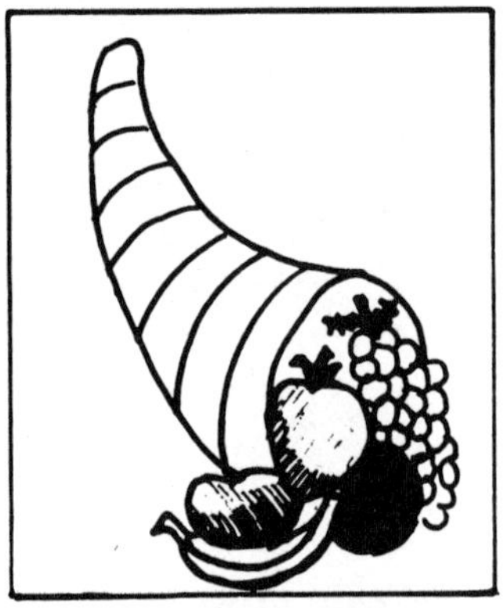

Materials

- magazines
- scissors, glue
- background paper for bulletin board

Directions

Teacher should attach a large cornucopia to background paper. Have children cut out various foods from magazines. Arrange the foods cascading out of the cornucopia.

Thanksgiving Placemat

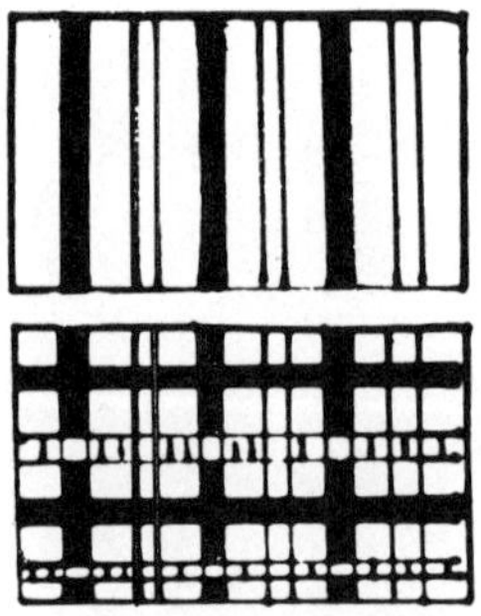

Materials

- 9" x 14" construction paper
- 9" various-colored paper strips
- glue

Directions

Glue strips vertically along placemat leaving spaces between the strips. Older children should be supplied with 14" strips as well so that their placement pattern could be both vertical and horizontal.

Harvest Paperweight

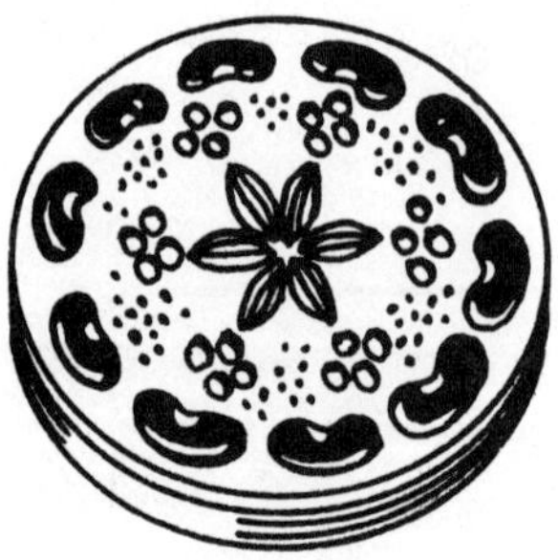

Concept

Textures can be seen and felt.

Materials

- plaster of Paris
- deep jar lids (mayonnaise, instant coffee, etc.)
- various seeds and dried beans
- felt

Directions

Give each child a lid. Mix plaster of Paris and pour immediately into each lid, filling almost to the top. As soon as plaster has been poured, instruct children to place beans in a design in the plaster. Let harden. Cover lid bottom and sides (if desired) with felt. (These make terrific holiday or special occasion gifts.)

DECEMBER IDEAS

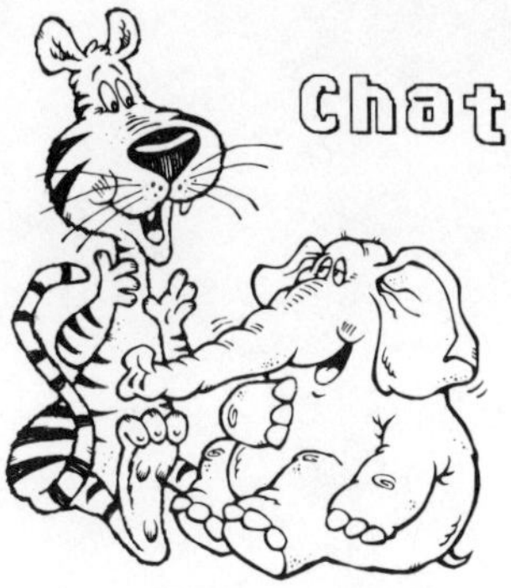

Chatter Box

One of the most important aspects of teaching art is putting the child at ease with a relaxed, positive, and caring attitude. It is up to the teacher to make these times ones of fun and sharing, thus creating an atmosphere conducive to learning.

Stained-Glass Murals

December Bulletin Board Idea

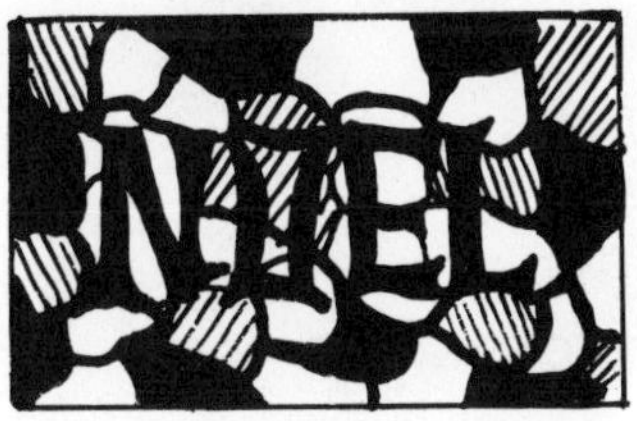

Materials

- precut paper sized to fit bulletin board
- tempera paint in various colors
- brushes

Directions

Lay large paper on floor. Draw large irregular shapes to resemble stained-glass. Have each child paint one shape. When complete and dry, teacher should outline each shape with black tempera paint. *(**Optional:** Large precut letters spelling out seasonal words may be centered on mural.)*

Stained-Glass Gift Jars

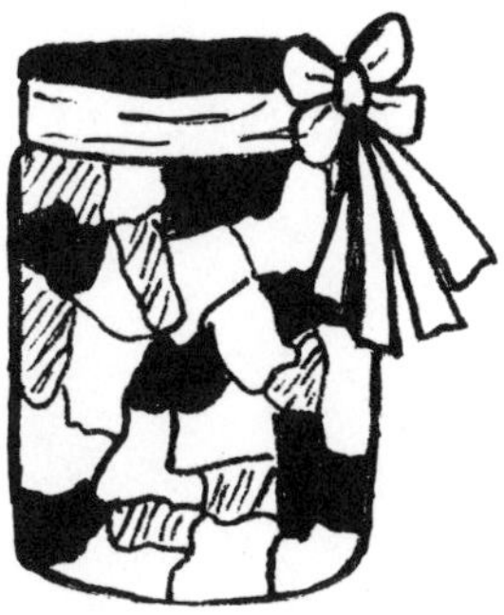

Materials

- small baby food jar with lid
- colored tissue paper, cut into small pieces
- paintbrush
- watered-down white glue (2 parts glue to 1 part water)
- *Optional trims*: felt, rickrack, lace, or ribbon

Directions

Using brush, glue tissue pieces to jar with watered-down glue, overlapping colors. When jar is covered completely, coat entire surface with glue again. Decorate lid with trims listed above. Fill with potpourri, or bath salts (recipe follows).

Recipe

Fill jar three-fourths full with epsom salts to which you may add perfume and/or food coloring. Replace lid and shake well.

Diamond-Shaped Santa

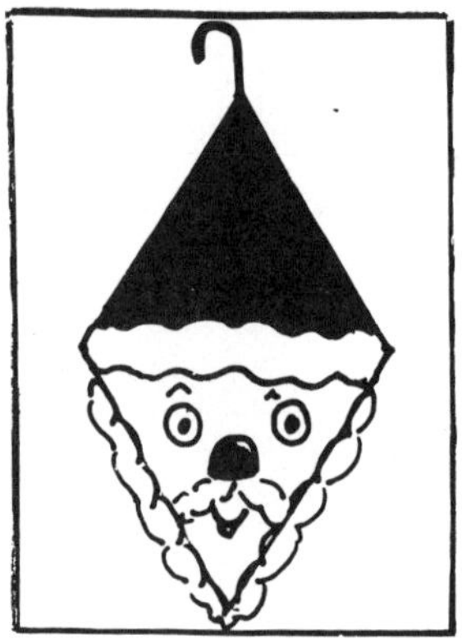

Materials

- metal clothes hanger
- nylon stocking
- red paper, felt, or cloth to fit hat
- scrap paper or fabric
- cotton
- glue, scissors

Directions

Stretch a nylon stocking over a hanger bent into a diamond shape. Glue fabric, paper, and cotton in place for features, hat, and beard. Hang Santa with the top hook in windows or around the classroom.

Triangle-Shaped Rudolf

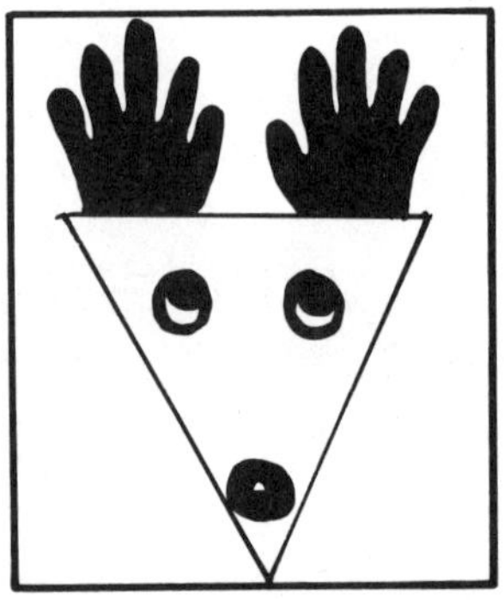

Materials

- Brown construction paper
- large triangle cardboard pattern for tracing
- scraps of black and red paper
- glue
- scissors

Directions

Trace triangle pattern on brown paper and cut out. Trace shape of child's hand twice and cut out. Glue two hand shapes on back upper edges of triangle for antlers. Cut large eyes out of black and a large red nose. Glue to triangle.

Motivation: The following poem may be used as motivation and/or follow-up for this project.

I am Rudolf, you can see
By the bright red nose you paste on me.
Add some eyes to my triangle face
Trace your hands and put them in place.
Now for Christmas, I'm ready to go
Hang me up so I will show.

Candy Cane Reindeer

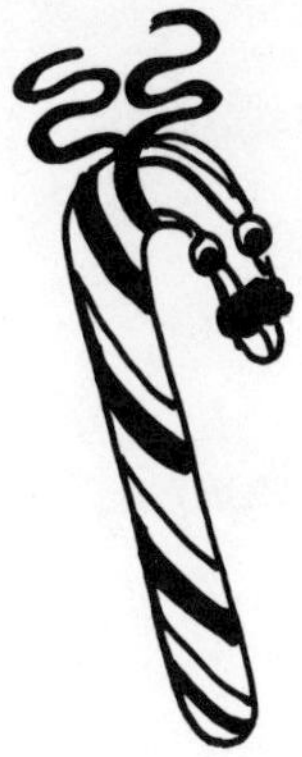

Materials

- medium-sized candy cane
- brown 12" pipe cleaner
- small red pom-pom
- pair of plastic movable eyes (1/4" diameter)
- glue

Directions

Leaving cellophane on candy cane, twist pipe cleaner around the top of the cane and then bend ends back and forth to form antlers. Glue pom-pom on tip for nose and eyes in between.

Salt Dough Ornaments

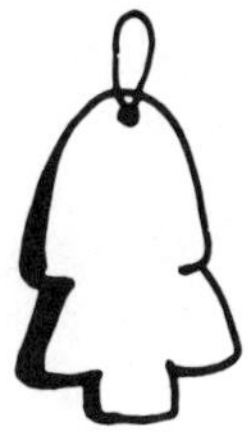

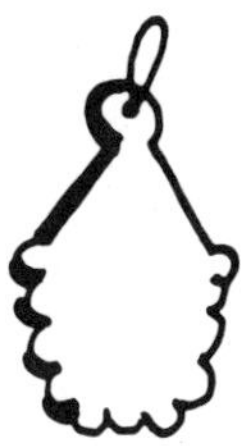

Recipe

1. Combine the following ingredients in this order.
   - 1 cup warm water
   - 1 cup salt
   - 2 cups flour

   (If precolored dough is desired, add vegetable dye to warm water.)
2. Blend well in a bowl, and knead as you would bread dough for at least 5 minutes.
3. Having each child work on a sheet of waxed paper, roll dough to about 1/4" and cut with Christmas cookie cutters into desired shapes.
4. Pierce top of each shape with pencil point. Through this hole, you may later insert ribbon or yarn for hanging.
5. Using a spatula, transfer ornaments from waxed paper to cookie sheet. (**Hint:** When transferring ornaments to cookie sheet, place a piece of masking tape on pan beneath each one with name of child written in ink.This will not burn when baked.)
6. Bake at 250 degrees for 1 1/2 to 2 hours or until hard to the touch.
7. After baking, name tapes can be put on the back of each ornament for easy identification.
8. If you have not dyed the dough, paint with tempera or liquid acrylic paints.
9. Spray fronts and backs with clear gloss acrylic sealer.

Paper Angel Ornament

Concept

Paper can be folded to make a 3-D shape.

Materials

- 9" x 6 " white construction paper
- half of a 6"- diameter paper doily
- 2" pink or white circle of construction paper
- yellow yarn
- glue
- stapler
- fine-tipped markers

Directions

Fold white paper accordian-fashion across the width of paper until it forms a fan. Pinch top of fan and staple together with a 6"- piece of looped yellow yarn (for hanging). On 2" pink circle, draw simple face and glue yellow yarn for hair. Glue face to top of fan. Glue the half doily on back of fan for wings.

Stuffed Ornament

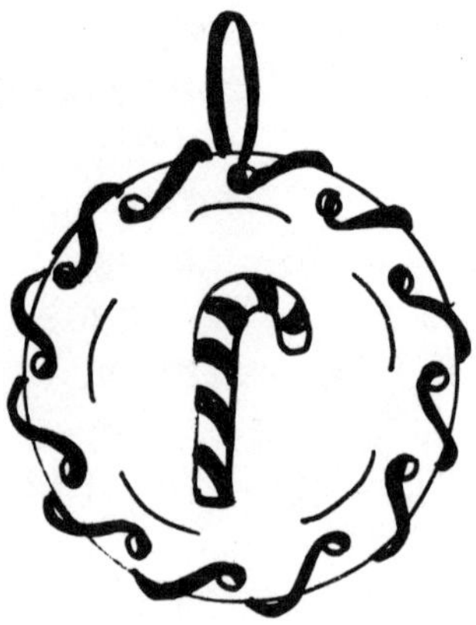

Materials

- white drawing paper
- red or green yarn
- crayons and/or glitter
- fiberfill (stuffing)
- hole punch
- shape patterns
- scissors

Directions

Trace the same shape twice on white paper and cut out. Holding the shapes together, punch holes around outside edge. Color one side of each. Begin to whipstitch the shapes with the yarn using fingers. Stuff loosely with fiberfill. Finish stitching and add a yarn loop for hanging. Now glitter can be added if desired.

Curly Christmas Tree

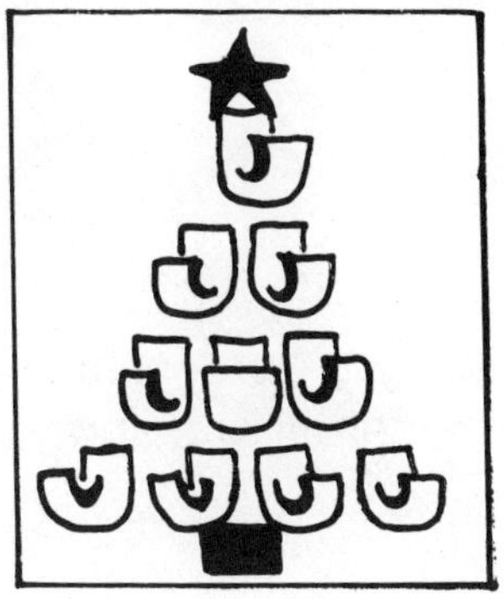

Concept

Rectangles can be rolled to form a curl; or shapes can be arranged to form a triangle. (This lesson also incorporates counting skills.)

Materials

- 1" x 6" green strips (10 per child)
- 1 small brown rectangle for trunk
- gold and silver scraps
- glitter or sequins
- fat pencils

Directions

Show how curls can be formed by rolling paper strips around a fat pencil or crayon. Have each child curl 10 strips. Starting with 1 curl for top, glue down all 10, adding 1 more curl to each line. Count these line by line when finished. Add trunk and decorate each curl with glitter or sequins.

Follow-up

Choose 10 children and ask them to position themselves like the pattern of curls on their tree. Ask these children to curl themselves like the paper.

Holiday Gift Bag and Card

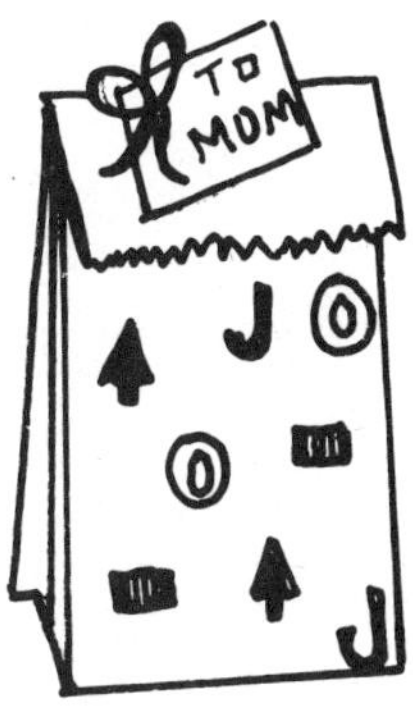

Materials

- brown or white lunch bag
- 2 1/2" square card
- red and green tempera (thick)
- printing objects—jar lids, corks, sponges, spools
- hole punch
- red and green yarn

Directions

Pour red and green paint in styrofoam trays lined with a paper towel. Using objects listed, print designs on bag and one small design on card. When dry, insert gift. Sign name to card. Fold down top of bag and punch a hole in center. Punch a hole in the card, pull yarn through both, and tie.

Photo and Frame

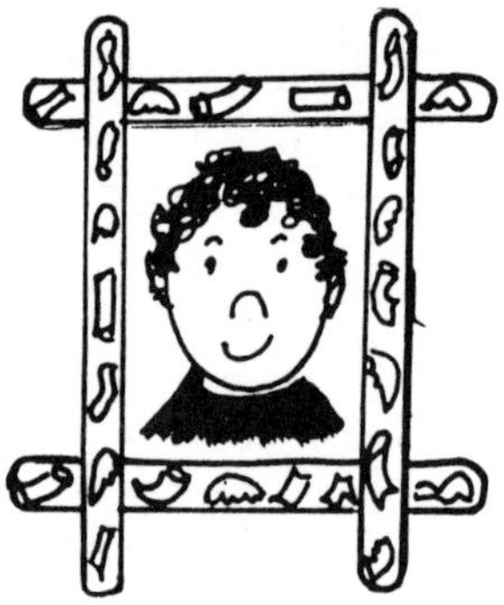

Materials

- snapshot of each child
- 4 wooden tongue depressors
- various shapes and sizes of macaroni
- glue
- gold spray paint
- picture hangers

Directions

Keeping your photo size in mind, glue tongue depressors together to form frame. Decorate with macaroni and spray gold. Glue photo to back of frame.

Pine Cone Reindeer

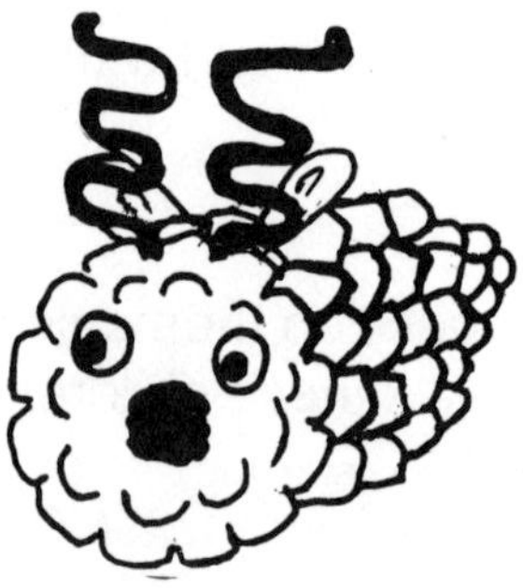

Materials:

- medium-sized pine cone
- 2 moveable eyes
- 1 brown 18" chenille stem
- small red chenille ball
- string or nylon thread for hanging
- glue

Directions:

Wrap chenille around middle of pine cone and twist. Bend ends back and forth to form antlers. Glue on eyes and red pom pom nose. Attach string for hanging.

Cutting on the Fold

The simplest cutting on the fold is done with very thin white paper folded just once. Have children fold a piece of paper in half. Then ask them to raise their left hands. Explain that this is the side on which the fold should be. Leaving paper flat on the table, have them draw half a circle. See if they can tell you why they are only drawing half of the circle and discuss this. Check each drawing first.

Then, keeping the paper folded, have them cut along the pencil line. Unfold each one to see the whole circle. This skill can be used for hearts, evergreen trees, snowmen, and many other symmetrical shapes and objects. Keep in mind the age of the group you are working with when choosing a shape for this practice work.

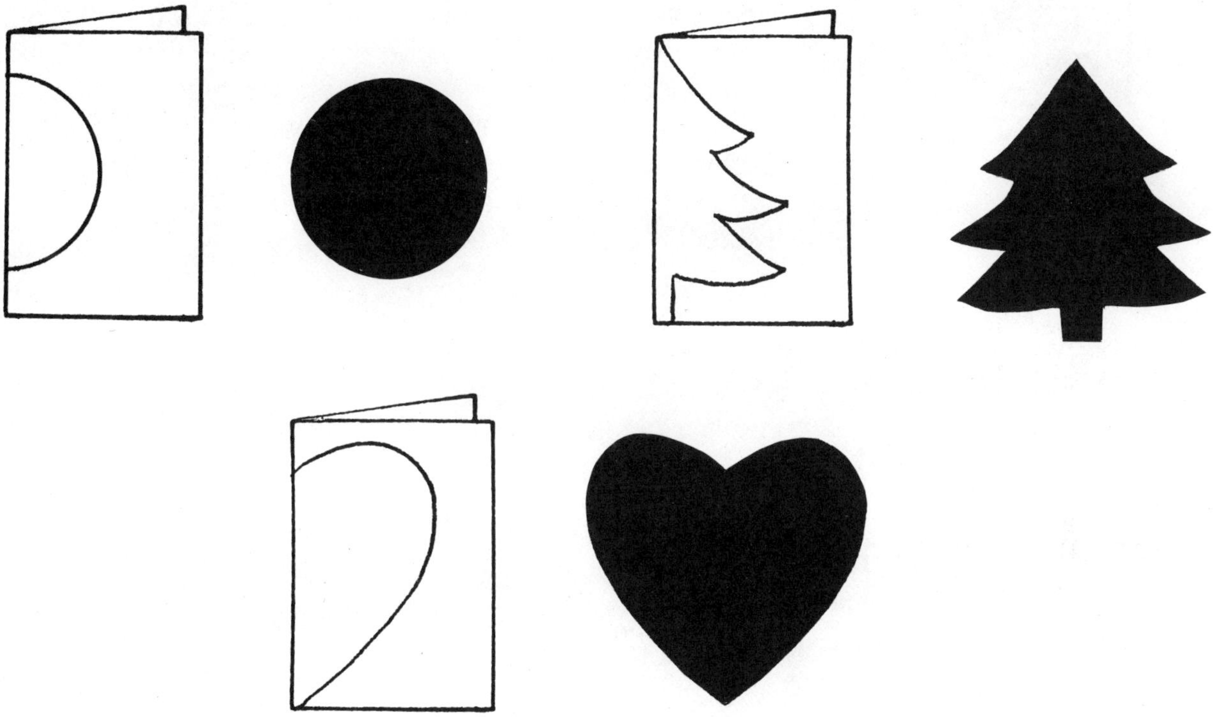

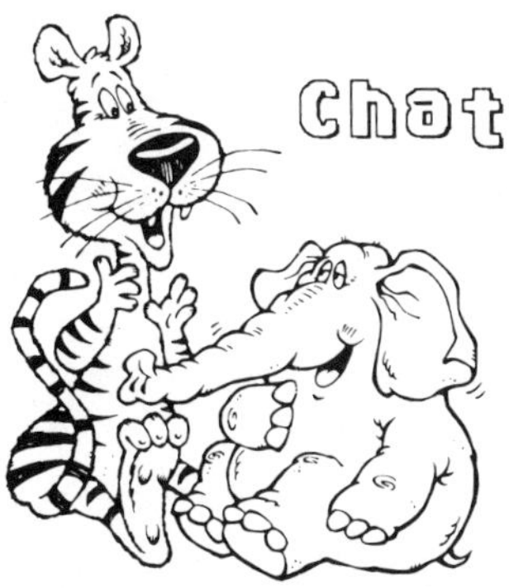

Chatter Box

Time for making things is not limited to an art period. Materials should be available for use throughout the day. Items children can work with or put together in their own ways are preferable. These may include crayons, paper, wood scraps, modeling clay, sand, seeds, and a variety of natural and recycled items.

Snowy Trees

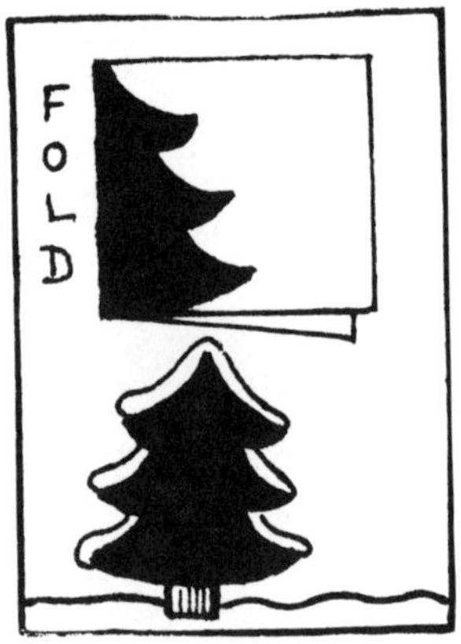

Concept

Paper can be cut on the fold to form a symmetrical object.

Materials

- 9" x 12" blue and green construction paper
- brown paper scraps
- raw cotton, cotton balls, or white tempera
- glue, pencil, scissors

Directions

Fold green paper the long way. Draw half a triangle fold (more experienced child can draw curving limbs). Keeping paper folded, cut out shape. Open and glue this to blue background paper. Glue small brown trunk shape at bottom of tree. Glue cotton on treetops, branches, and around bottom of tree for snowy effect. Variations for snow: white tempera or white chalk.

White Lace Designs

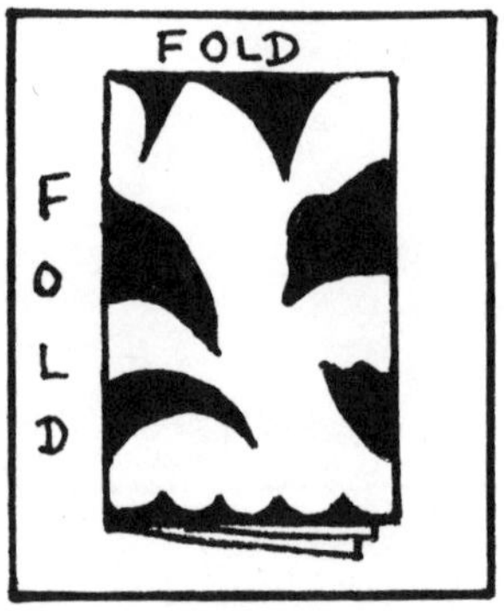

Concept

Paper can be cut on the fold to form lacy designs.

Materials

- newsprint paper for practice
- 9" x 12" background construction paper
- 9" x 12" thin white paper
- glue, scissors

Directions

Fold newsprint paper into quarters. Practice cutting in on all sides toward the center of the fold. When successful lacy designs are achieved, have group repeat this using good white paper. Glue finished product to background or hang in windows or from ceiling.

Grandma's Quilt

Motivation: Bring in a patchwork quilt and place it on the floor.Have children sit around it. Discuss why quilts are and were made of many different pieces of material. Look at these pieces and talk about the patterns they form. Each individual piece also may contain patterns of dots, lines, colors, motifs, etc.

Concept

Shapes can be combined to form patterns

Materials

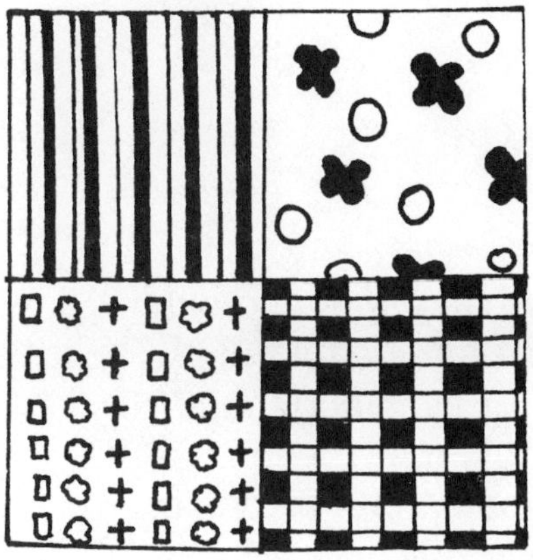

- 6" x 6" piece of white or light-colored construction paper for each child
- felt markers or crayons
- large piece of background paper big enough to accommodate each child's square

Optional Materials

- 6" x 6" piece of white or light-colored fabric cut with pinking shears
- felt markers, fabric crayons, or liquid embroidery

Directions

Have each child make a pattern on a paper or fabric square. Assemble squares to form a quilt—paper squares are glued onto background paper, and fabric squares can be stitched together with or without a large piece of fabric backing or glued to background paper.

Winter Tree

Concept

Spatter painting makes use of manipulative skills.

Materials

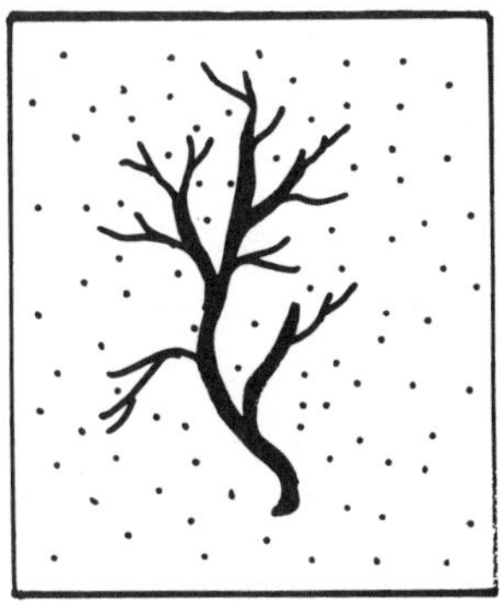

- evergreen or small twig
- 9" x 12" dark blue paper for background
- white tempera paint
- metal or plastic screening
- shallow carton (to prevent splattering surroundings)
- toothbrush or vegetable brush
- clear tape

Directions

Tape tree to middle of blue background paper and place inside shallow carton. Cover with screen. Dip small brush into paint and rub it back and forth across screen to make snow.

Snowman Mobile

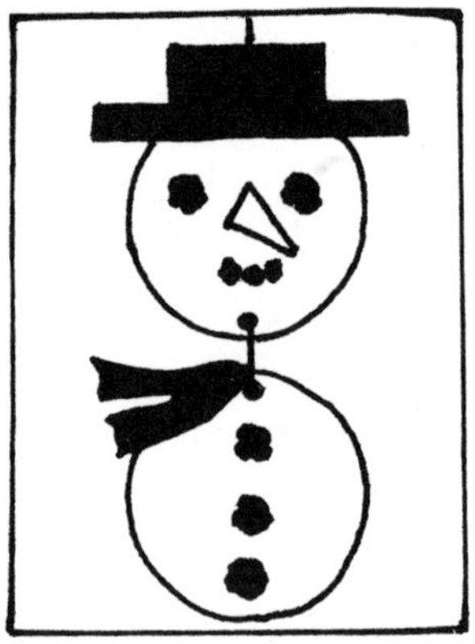

Concept

Shapes can be assembled to move when suspended.

Materials

- one 6 1/2" and one 8" circle pattern for tracing
- white and orange construction paper
- 4" x 4 1/2" rectangle and 1" x 8" strip of black construction paper
- black tissue paper scraps
- fabric scraps
- yarn
- hole punch
- pencils, glue, scissors

Directions

Using circle patterns, trace both on white paper and cut out. Punch a hole at top of large circle and bottom of smaller circle. Crumple black tissue for eyes and mouth and glue to smaller circle. Cut a triangle (carrot) nose from orange paper and glue on face. Crumple three pieces of tissue paper for buttons and glue on large circle. Attach larger circle to smaller one with yarn, leaving some space between the two. Tie a 16" piece of yarn in top hole of snowman and secure for hanging. Glue black rectangle and strip on head to form hat. Add a fabric scrap for a scarf at top of body. Hang when displaying. (This project may take two sessions.)

Personalized Snowflake

Motivation: Discuss snowflakes with the group, explaining that all snowflakes have six points and that no two are exactly alike. Show pictures if possible.

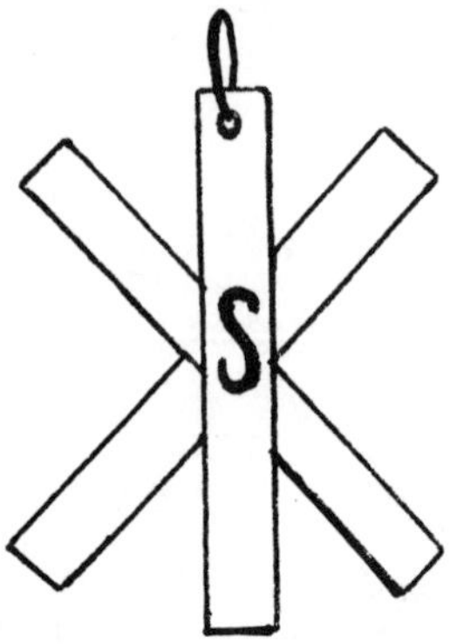

Concept

Shapes can be overlapped to form a new shape.

Materials

- three 9" x 1" white strips of construction paper per child
- glitter
- glue
- string
- hole punch

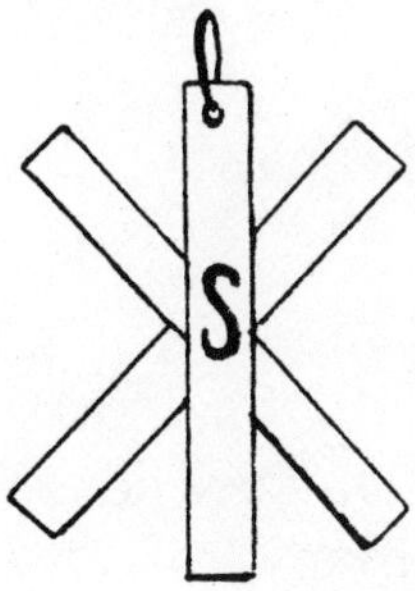

Directions

Glue one white strip on top of another to form an "X." Glue the third strip in the middle of the "X." The teacher or the child may then draw the initial of his/her first name in the center of the snowflake with glue. Cover with glitter. Punch a hole in the top strip and insert string for hanging.

Snowman Stencil Print

Concept

A stencil can be used to form a print.

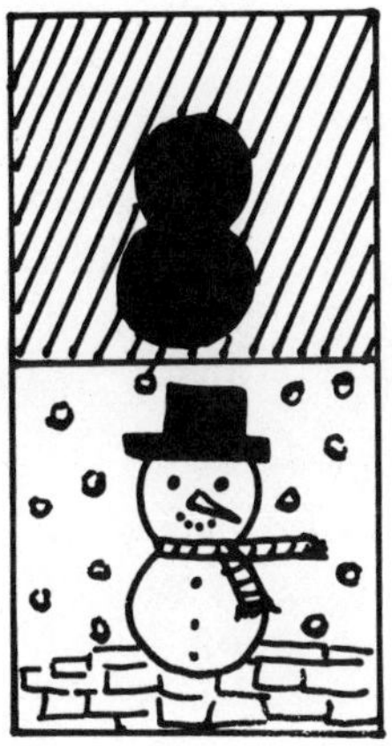

Materials

- 9" x 12" poster board
- 9" x 12" blue paper for background
- white tempera paint
- sponges
- scrap box
- small black beans
- glue, scissors

Directions

Day One —Cut a snowman silhouette in the center of the poster board. Remove stencil when complete. Dab sponge in the white tempera paint and sponge snow underneath the snowman. Using corner of sponge, print snowflakes around snowman. Let dry.

Day Two —Decorate snowman with beans for eyes, mouth, and buttons. Cut hat, nose, and scarf out of scrap paper and glue into place.

Motivation: The following song may be used as motivation and/or follow-up for the next two projects. (Sung to the tune of "Twinkle, Twinkle Little Star.")

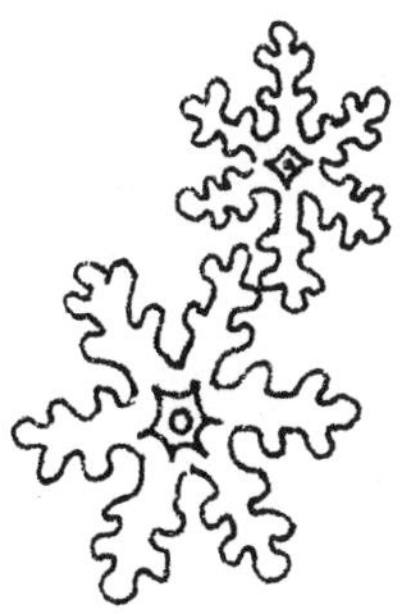

Winter Towns

Snow is falling on our town,
On the roofs and on the ground
Chimney tops and cars and streets
In the park where children meet.
Now it covers everything.
Oh what fun the snow will bring!

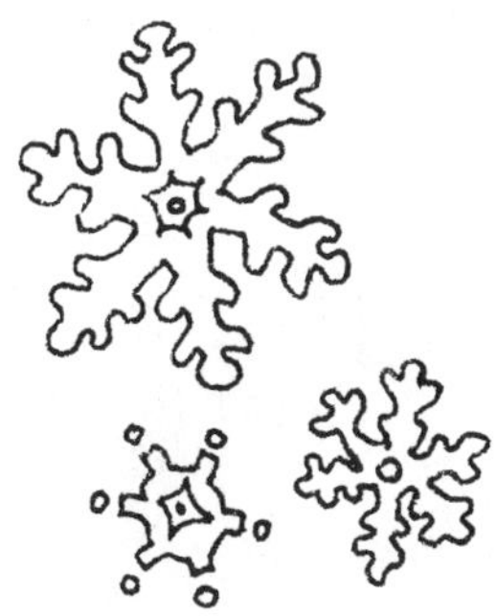

Crayon and Tempera Town

(Recommended for kindergarten age or older)

Motivation: Talk with children about where they live—in a city, in the suburbs, in a town, on a farm, etc. What kinds of buildings are there where they live? Do they have windows? Doors? Are the streets busy or quiet or tree-lined? Are there many trees or bushes or streams or ponds? Where would snow land if it fell where they live?

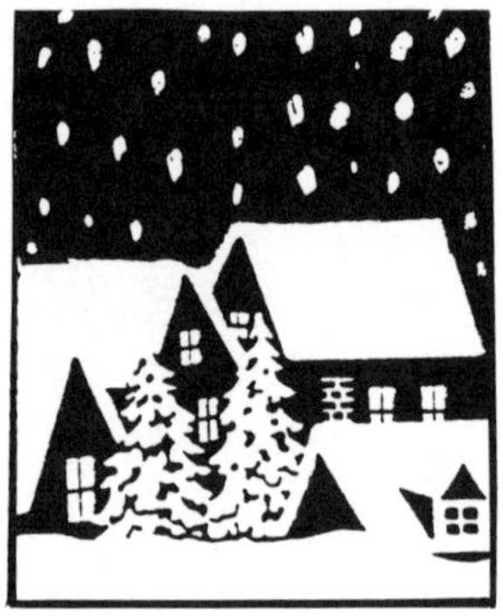

Materials

- 12" x 18" manila drawing paper
- crayons
- white tempera paint
- paintbrushes

Directions

Draw a picture of your town, city, or home with crayons. Be sure to bear down hard to make your picture bright and colorful. Include as many details as you can to make it interesting. With white tempera, cover the rooftops, trees, buildings, sidewalks, etc., for a snowy look. Dots of paint can show the snow falling from the sky. Works by such artists as Currier and Ives and Grandma Moses can be used with this lesson.

Milk Carton Town

This is a long-term class project. It is recommend that the teacher paint the milk cartons for younger groups. The town can be assembled on a large piece of heavy cardboard, plywood, or masonite.

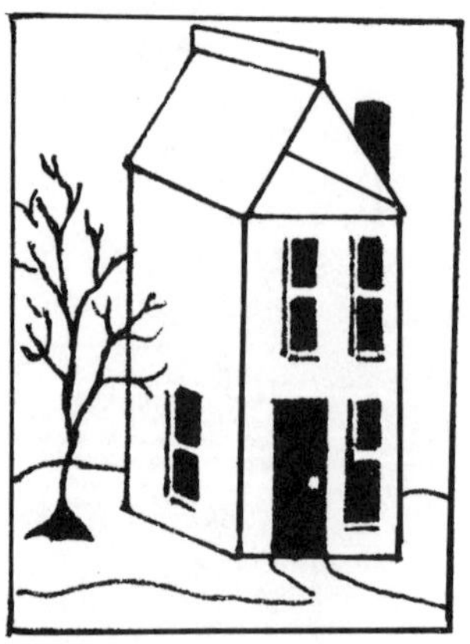

Materials

- milk cartons of various sizes with openings taped shut
- white tempera
- construction paper
- raw cotton or cotton balls
- modeling clay
- twigs or small tree branches
- glue, scissors, brushes

Directions

Paint all cartons with two coats of white tempera. Let dry. Cut shapes for windows and doors from construction paper and glue on cartons. Glue houses to platform. Add streets and sidewalks with construction paper. Set twigs into small mounds of modeling clay and place around town. Cover rooftops, ground, and trees with cotton. Children may add small figures and cars from home if desired.

Snow Deer

Motivation: Read the book *Fergus and the Snow Deer* by Yasuko Kimura.

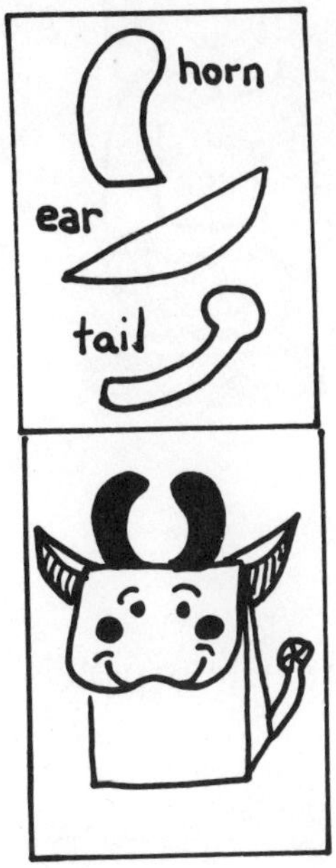

Materials
- white paper bags (brown bags painted white can be used)
- light blue, white, and purple construction paper
- marking pens
- glue, scissors
- precut patterns for ears, horns, and tail (for younger children)

Directions

Read and show pictures from Kimura's book listed above. (If your local library does not have this book, make up your own story about a snow deer.) Cut (or trace and cut) blue ears, purple horns, and a white tail. Round off top corners of paper bag. Fold top down about 3". Glue horns to top of head, ears on back of bag, and tail near the bottom.Add face with marking pens, including pink cheeks.

Footprint Snow Creature

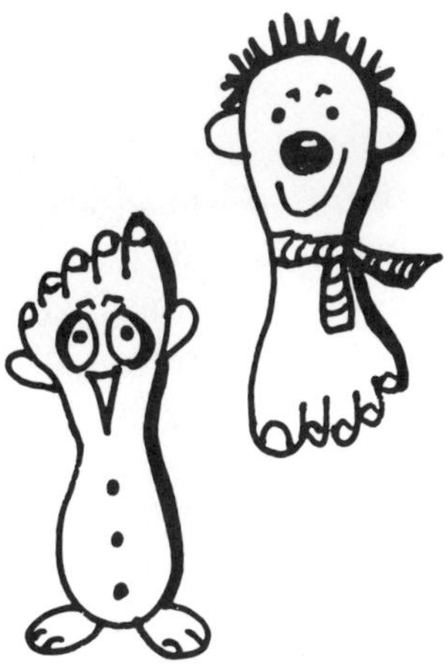

Concept

This activity encourages creativity and imagination.

Materials
- white tempera paint on tray
- 9" x 12" dark-colored construction paper
- scrap box
- marking pens
- glue, scissors
- pail of water and paper towels

Directions

Place bare foot in tempera paint and press in middle of dark paper. Immediately wash foot in pail and dry with towels. Let print dry. Discuss all kinds of features that could be used in creating a snow creature such as: claws, paws, hands, beaks, noses, wings, tails, scales, ears, antennae, etc. Add features using markers and/or paper scraps.

Motivation: Use this poem for motivation and/or follow-up with the next project.

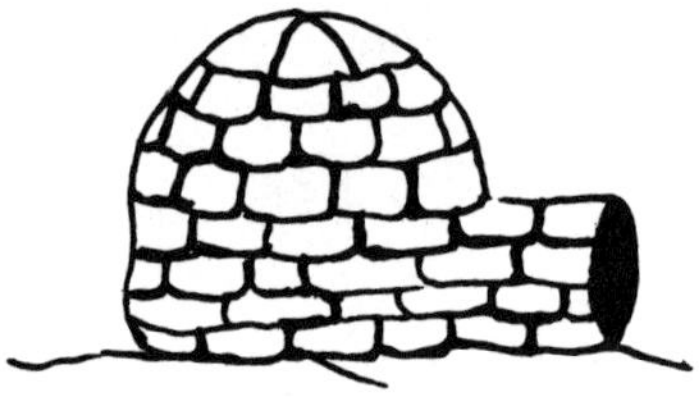

Here is my Eskimo
For all of you to meet.
He wears a furry jacket
And warm boots upon his feet.

His cheeks are rosy from the cold.
His tiny nose is too.
He has a great big friendly smile
Especially for you.

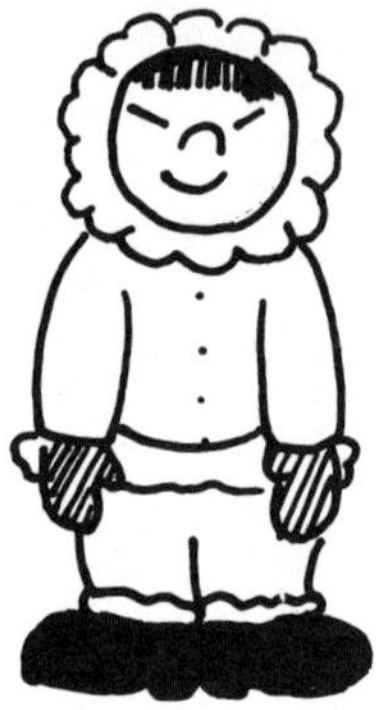

Eskimo Puppet

Motivation: Discuss people who live where it is cold most of the time. Show pictures, if possible, of Eskimos and the way they dress for the cold.

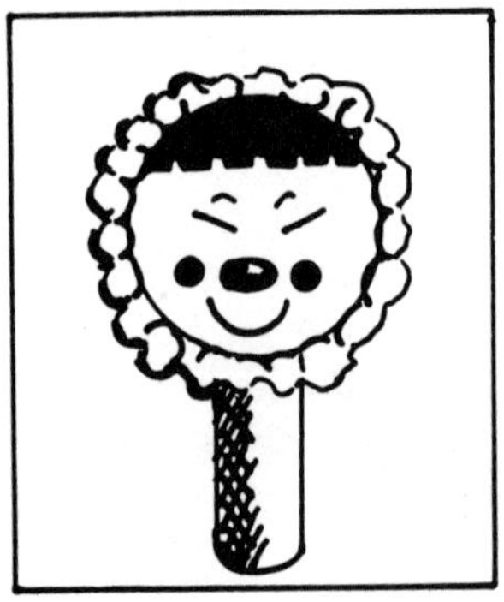

Materials

- wooden craft stick
- 3 1/2" tagboard circle
- black construction paper scraps
- pink tissue scraps
- cotton
- marking pens
- glue, scissors

Directions

Fringe black strip of construction paper. Glue to top of circle for hair. Trim edges even with circle. Draw face with marking pens and glue pink crumpled tissue nose in place. Surround circle with cotton for fur hood. Glue circle to stick.

Printing Techniques and Procedures

Printing is a unique art activity because it is filled with surprise and suspense. No one ever knows exactly what the end result will be. Small children are fascinated by the systematic procedures and often amazed by the product. Also, repeating a single design appeals to their sense of rhythm. Have some fun with the following activities.

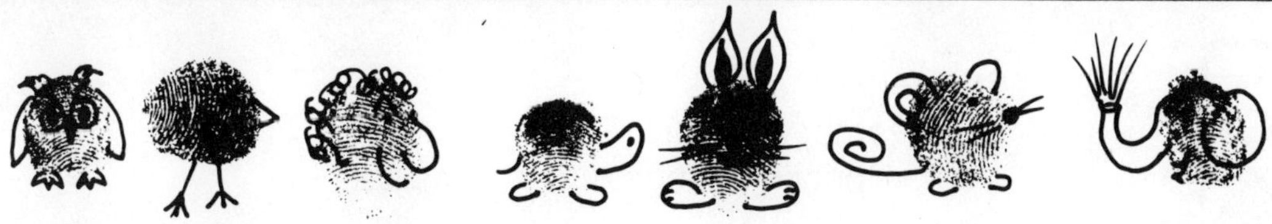

Potato Chalk Prints: Cut potato in half. Rub cut surface thoroughly with colored chalk and print. Keep wet paper towel or sponge nearby to dampen potato before re-applying chalk.

Gadget Printing on Unusual Surfaces: Use sponges, jar lids, spools, corks, wood, walnut halves, cardboard edges, etc., to print on such varied surfaces as tissue, newspaper, paper towel, paper plates, cloth, and burlap.

Fingerpaint Print: Using hands, wrist, fist, and/or fingers, spread fingerpaint on tabletop or tray. Press the paper flat on top of design to create a monoprint (a single print).

Stencil Prints: Cut a silhouette from the center of a piece of cardboard. Place on paper and dab tempera paint inside the form with a sponge.

Pipe Cleaner Prints: Twist several pipe cleaners into different shapes, bending up one end for a handle. Dip shapes into paint and print.

Modeling Clay Print: Coat clay with liquid detergent so water-base paint will adhere. Flatten clay and press designs in it with a pencil or blunt tool. Apply tempera paint to clay design with a brush. Press paper on clay to print.

Helpful Hints for Printmaking

1. Write name on all printing paper first.
2. Pour fairly thick tempera in a styrofoam tray lined with a paper towel.
3. To make a handle for printing objects, glue a spool on top.
4. Demonstrate and emphasize the "down-up" motion used in many printing processes.
5. Remind children to use only one color of paint per object so as to prevent color mixing.

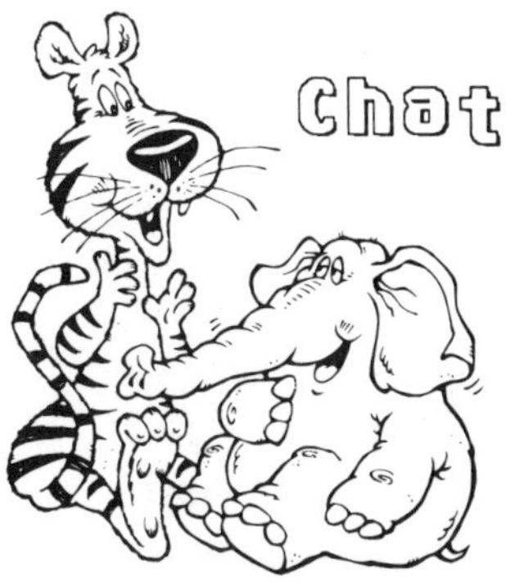

Chatter Box

It is sometimes appropriate to hold up a child's art work for the whole class to see. Be specific as to the reason. For example, when making gadget prints, a specific comment could be "I like the way you've repeated that shape, Nancy. You've shown movement by repeating it."

FEBRUARY IDEAS

Gadget Print Patterns

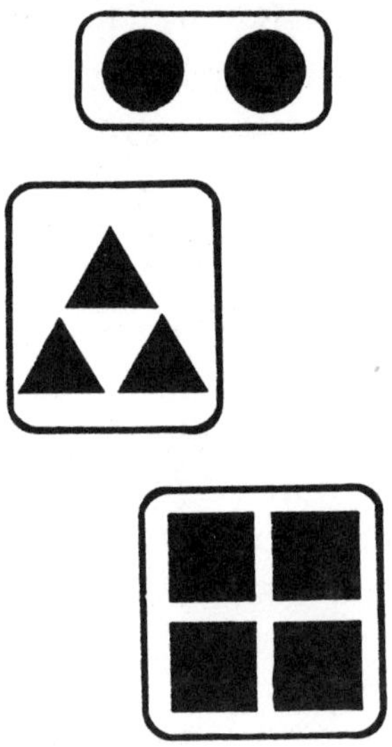

Concept

Patterns can be made by repeating shapes. (This is a good readiness activity in visual patterning and counting.)

Materials

- tempera paint
- 3 printing gadgets (see page 33)
- paper
- samples of patterned wallpaper, jewelry, fabric, etc.

Directions

Discuss what is meant by a "pattern" and show samples like those listed above. Using paints and gadgets, demonstrate a printed pattern by repeating and alternating shapes. For example:

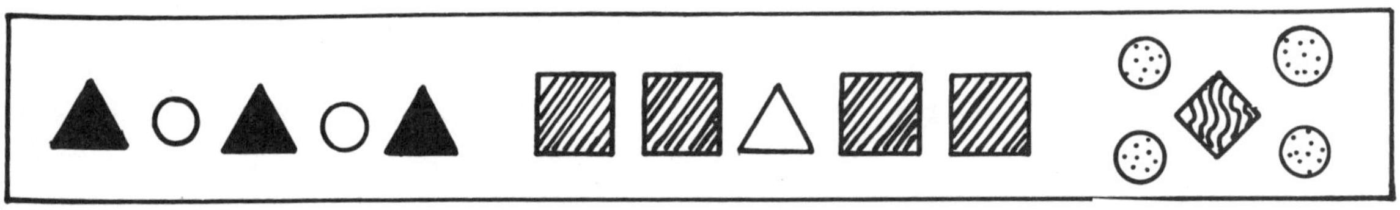

Melted Crayon Print

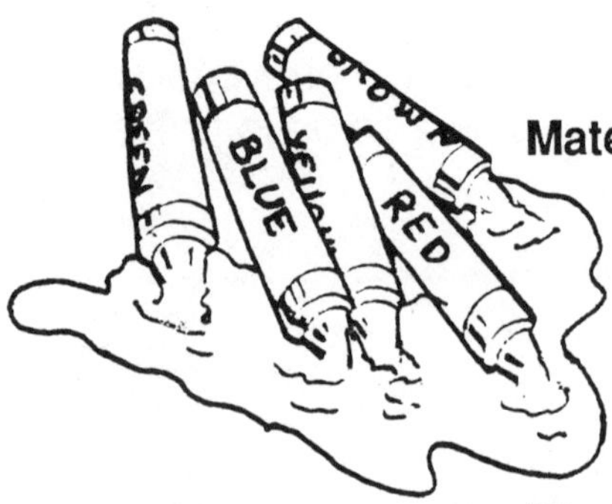

Concept

An image can be transferred from one surface to another to produce a print.

Materials

- electric warming tray
- oven mitt
- aluminum foil
- peeled crayons
- paper

Directions

Cover warming tray surface with a piece of aluminum foil. Allow tray to heat up. Draw a design using several crayon colors on the foil. Watch as crayons melt on warm surface. Lay paper over melted design. The teacher presses paper using oven mitt. Lift print. Wipe off foil with a paper towel for the next child. These designs should delight the whole class.

Hearts, Hearts, Hearts

Concept
Heart creatures can be made by combining different-size hearts. Below are five ideas you may wish to apply.

Materials
- construction paper in assorted colors
- crayons or felt markers
- scissors, glue

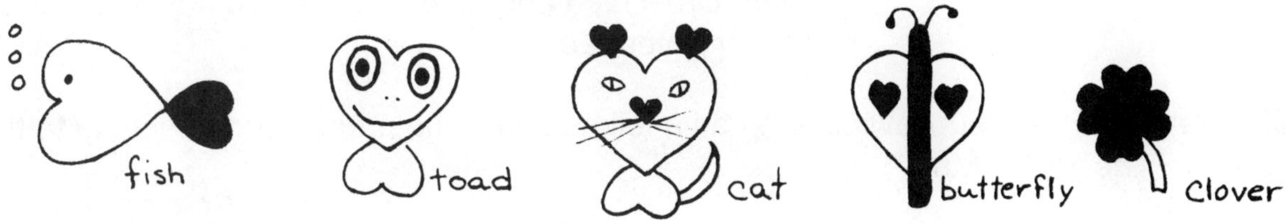

The Loving Tree

February Bulletin Board Idea

Motivation: Use this poem as motivation and/or follow-up for the following project. It could be placed beneath the completed class project. Paint or cut a large tree with branches and place on bulletin board.

The Loving Tree

We all have made this loving tree
Filled with hearts, so gay.
It shows the names of those we love
In a very special way.

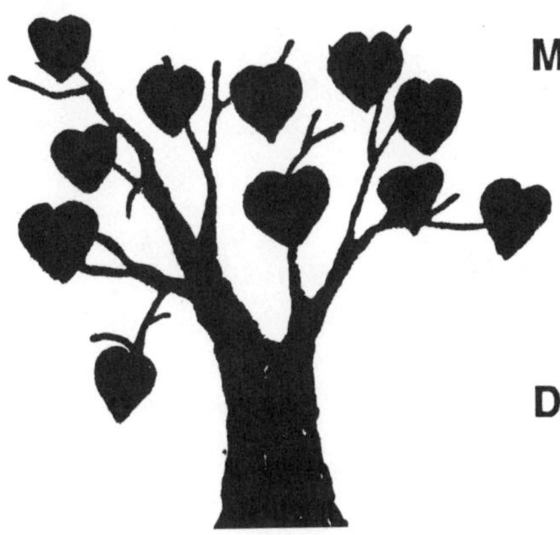

Materials
- a large painted tree with many branches
- 4" heart patterns
- 6" x 4 1/2" red construction paper
- black marking pens
- scissors, glue

Directions
Trace heart pattern on red construction paper and cut out. Have each child tell you the name of a person he or she loves. With marker, write "I love ____________" on each heart or have the children help decorate the "Loving Tree."

Loving Bug

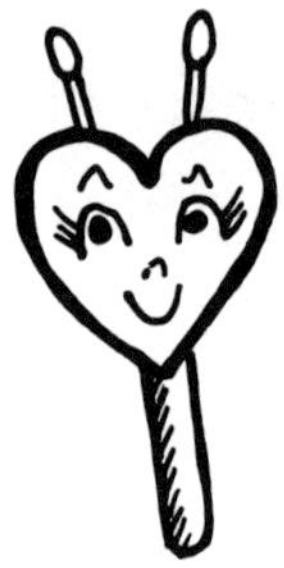

Materials

- small wooden ice cream spoon (or tongue depressor)
- 1 cotton swab cut in half
- marking pens
- 3" red paper square
- glue, scissors

Directions

Cut heart on fold of red paper square. Glue spoon in center of heart. Draw face and glue cotton swab halves behind spoon for antennae.

Motivation: Use the following song as a follow-up for the project above. (Sung to the tune of "The Muffin Man.")

Loving Bug

Do you know the loving bug, the loving bug, the loving bug?
Do you know the loving bug,
Who comes on Valentine's Day?

He comes to give a kiss & hug, a kiss & hug, a kiss & hug
He comes to give a kiss & hug
To [insert child's name] on Valentine's Day.

Note:

Use as many of the children's names in the second verse as you have time for.

Blot-Print Valentine

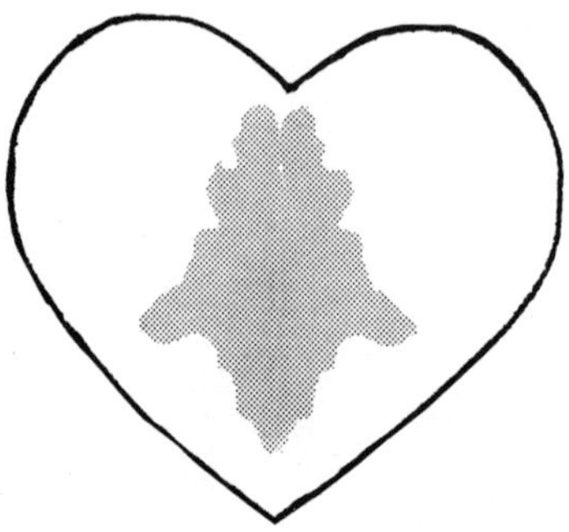

Concept

Two colors can be mixed to form a new color.

Materials

- white heart (cut on fold from 9" x 12" white paper)
- red and white tempera paint
- brushes
- scissors

Directions

Open paper heart and drop two blobs of white tempera and two blobs of red tempera on one side of the paper. Re-fold paper and press together. Open and make note of the new color that appears.

Fingerpainted Valentines

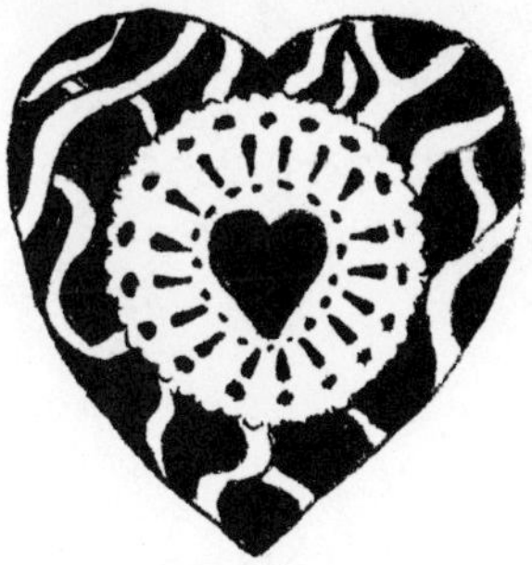

Concept

Various media can be combined to make a valentine.

Materials

- red and white fingerpaint
- fingerpaint paper
- 6" round or heart-shaped doily
- red construction paper
- glue, scissors

Directions

Day One —Place a dab of red and white fingerpaint on wet paper for each child. Have child spread the paint over paper, mixing colors and creating an interesting design. Use all parts of hands for this—palm, fist, spread fingers, heel of palm, and fingertips. Let dry.

Day Two —Fold dry fingerpainting in half. Draw half of a heart on this, and cut it out along pencil line. Open and glue doily in center of heart. Using red construction paper, cut a smaller heart on the fold and glue in the center of the doily.

3-D Hearts

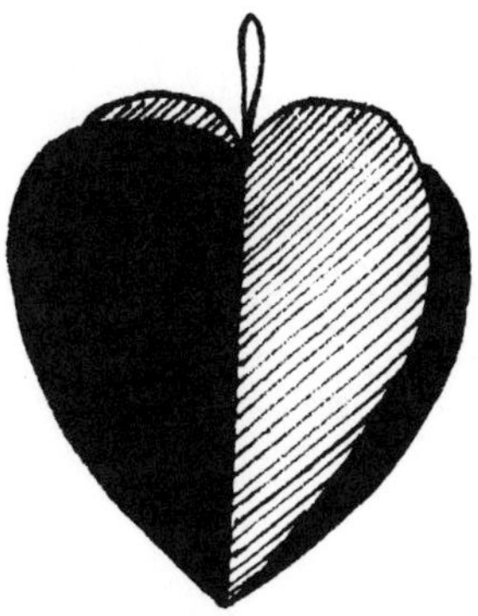

Concept

Flat shapes can be made into three-dimensional shapes.

Materials

- red construction paper
- thread or thin string
- glitter
- glue, pencil, scissors, hole punch

Directions

Fold paper in half. Draw half a heart. Cut along line, open, and repeat so that you have two hearts of the same size. Slit one heart half-way down from the top. Slit second heart half-way up from the bottom. (See diagram.) Punch a hole in top of second heart. Then, as the children decorate both hearts with glitter, the teacher may tie a string through each heart with the hole. Slip hearts together at slits. Hang around the room or from a bare tree branch. Teacher may want to draw lines for slits so that the children will know exactly where to cut.

Patriotic Weaving

Motivation: Discuss weaving—combining pieces of straw, fabric, paper, yarn, string, or thread in an over-under process. Name some things made from woven materials such as rugs, baskets, cloth, and placemats.

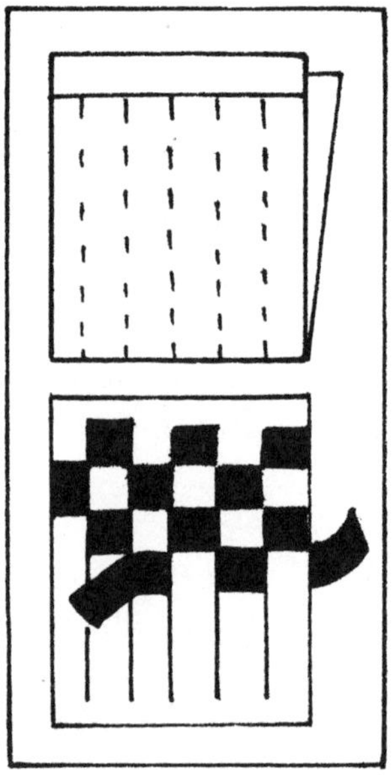

Materials

- 9" x 12" blue construction paper
- three 1 1/2" x 9" strips of white construction paper
- three 1 1/2" x 9" strips of red construction paper
- a 1 1/2" x 9" cardboard ruler
- pencil, scissors, glue

Directions

Fold blue paper in half. Place flat on table so that fold is facing child. Place cardboard ruler at the very top of the open side, and draw a horizontal line straight across. Draw five vertical lines starting from the top line, using width of the ruler (see drawing #1). Keeping paper folded, cut along each vertical line, being sure to stop at top horizontal line. Open. You are now ready to weave white and red strips alternately in an over-under pattern through the blue paper. Explain to the child that the weaving should look like a checkerboard. When complete, glue down ends.

Note

Make sure that if you start "over" on the first strip that you start "under" on the second.

Lincoln's Log Cabin

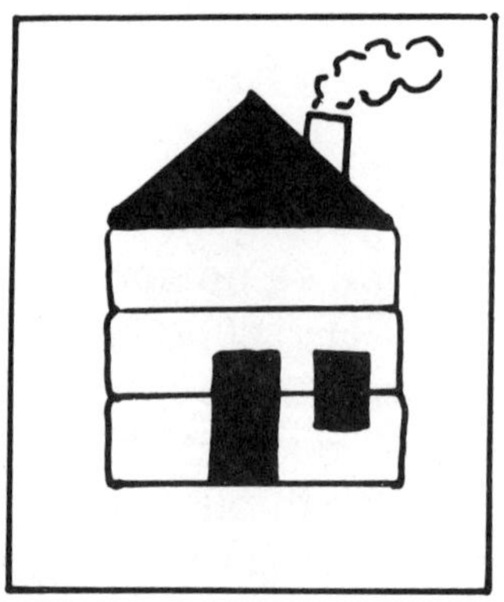

Concept

Shapes can be combined to form a recognizable object.

Materials

- three 1" x 5" cardboard strips
- 9" x 12" construction paper for background
- 5"- base construction paper triangle
- cotton
- paper scrap box
- glue, scissors

Directions

Build a log cabin by gluing cardboard strips on background paper. Add triangle roof and rectangle door and chimney. Glue cotton on top of chimney for smoke.

An Imaginative Look at Painting

Make painting an exciting event in your classroom. Painting can let imaginations soar when ordinary materials are used in out-of-the-ordinary ways. Be willing to take chances and be experimental. The results will be fun, rewarding, and revealing. The following process-oriented activities provide opportunities for discovery and problem solving.

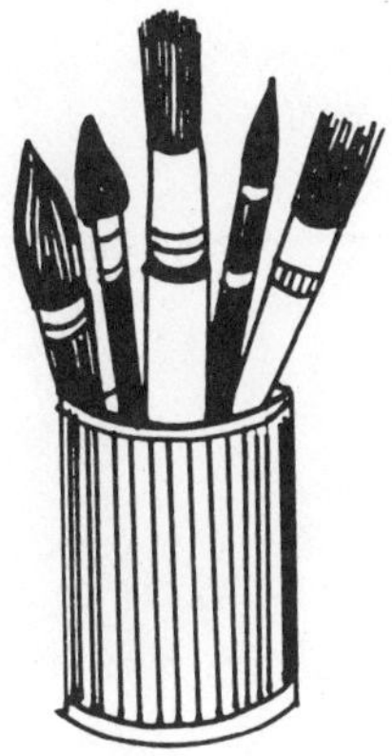

A Bucket of Brushes: Fill a container with several sizes of brushes—1/2", 1", 2", 4", and even 5". Make sure each child knows that it is all right to use any or all sizes for the painting. Fill a mixing bowl or large coffee can with tempera paint, and observe the choice of brushes each child makes.

Musical Mural: Cut a large sheet of mural paper (enough for the whole class) and place on floor. Group children around paper. Pour small amounts of one color (for whole class) of tempera into tuna cans (These are low and won't topple easily). Select a classical record that evokes a specific mood or feeling, and direct the children to paint to the music.

Painting on Free Forms: Traditional easel painting always assumes that rectangular paper will be used. Try this experiment. Cut or tear one, two, or all corners of easel paper off in unusual ways. Present this irregularly shaped paper to the children, saying nothing. See if they take this unusal paper shape into consideration as they paint. Some children will respond to the shape, while others may ignore it.

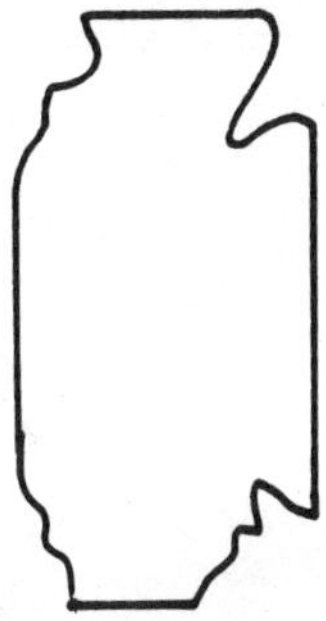

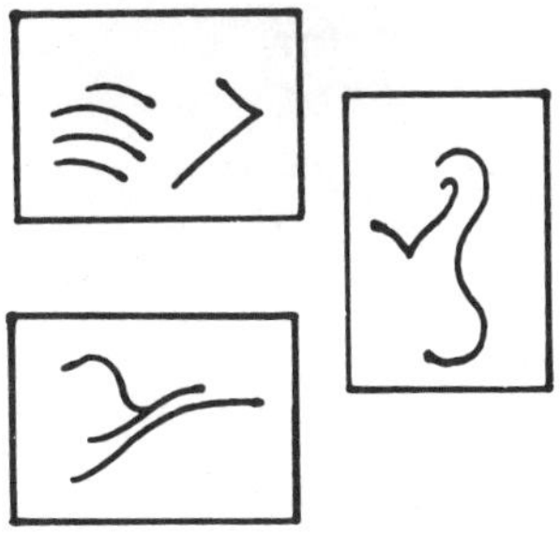

Painting on Marked Paper: The teacher should place a few marks with paint on paper, preparing one sheet for each child. The marks can be varied or imaginative (see sketch). Now let each child choose the marked paper that appeals to him. Watch as he copes with your markings to create his own imaginative painting. Did he ignore your marks or incorporate them into his design?

Painting Around a Problem: Cut a shape out of the middle of a folded piece of easel paper. (Older children can prepare the paper themselves.) Open paper. Notice the negative space now in the middle. Place on newspaper. Watch the child solve the problem of painting around this negative space. The results will be unique.

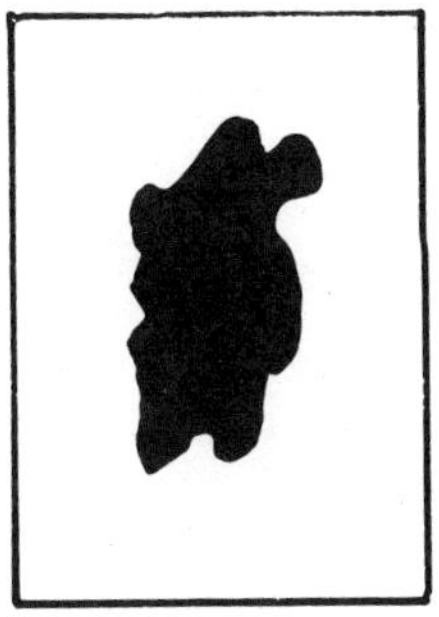

MARCH IDEAS

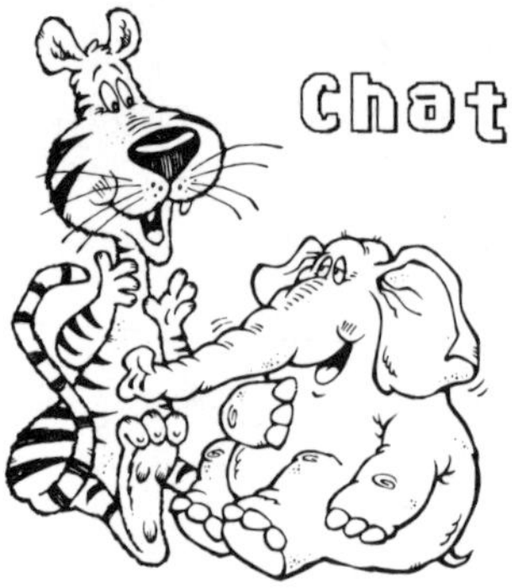

Chatter Box

It is important for the chosen activity to be suitable to the child's developmental level. Disinterest may indicate a lack of readiness. Choose only those activities that can provide a feeling of success and accomplishment.

Pastel Marble Print

Motivation: Review how adding white to a color changes its value. This would be a good time to introduce the word "pastel." This activity utilizes only pastel colors, which could be mixed as the children watch.

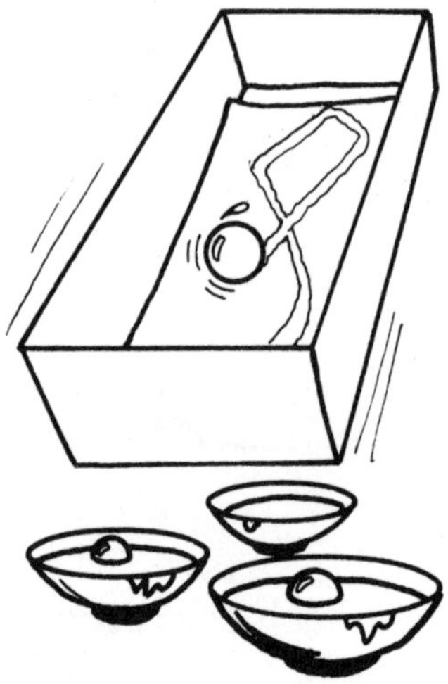

Materials

- pink, light green, light blue tempera
- 3 bowls
- 3 spoons
- 3 marbles
- shoe box
- white paper cut to cover shoe box

Directions

Place paper inside box. Dip one marble in one color. Remove with spoon and place it in the box. Roll marble around inside the box and remove. Repeat with all the colors.

Pastel Painting

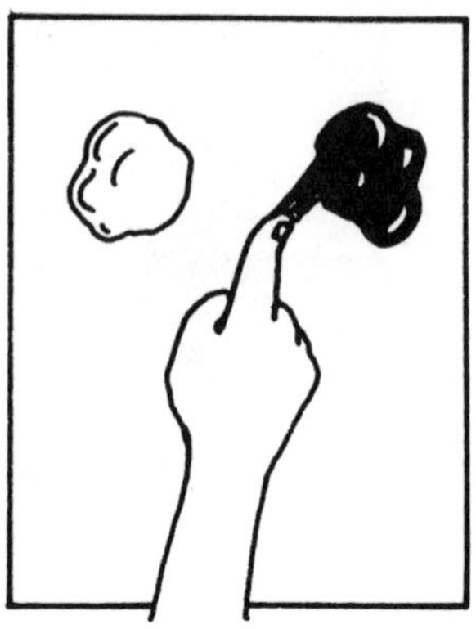

Concept

Two colors can be mixed to form a third color.

Materials

- blue and white fingerpaint
- fingerpaint paper

Directions

Place 1 tbls. of each color of fingerpaint on paper. Fingerpaint a design combining colors. Let dry.

Motivation: The following poem can be used as motivation and/or follow-up for the next two projects.

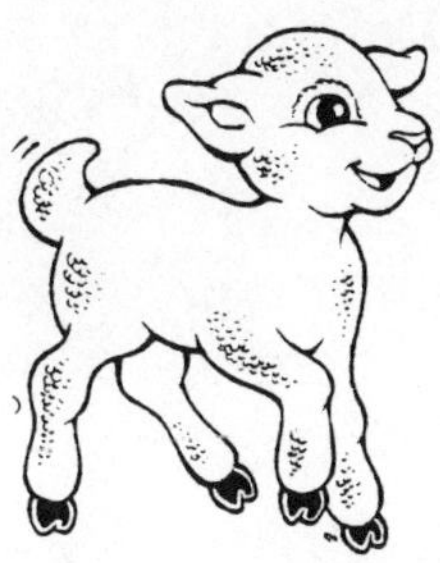

When March comes in like a lion
The cold winds bluster and blow
But when March days are over
Like a lamb they softly go.

When March comes in like a lamb
The sun is warm and bright
But then when March is over
The roaring lion comes into sight.

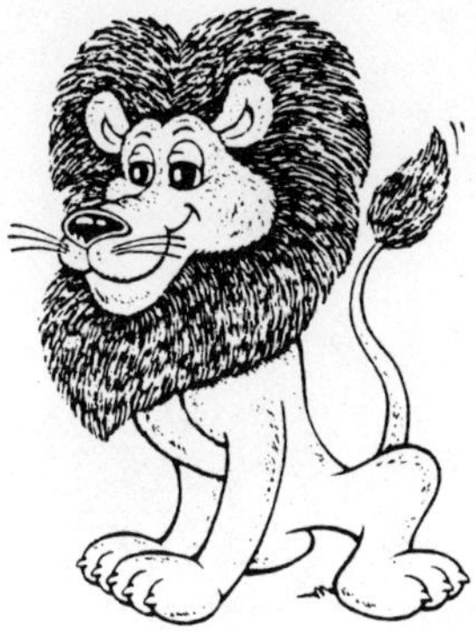

The Lion of March

Concept

Paper can be sculpted to form a two-dimensional shape.

Materials

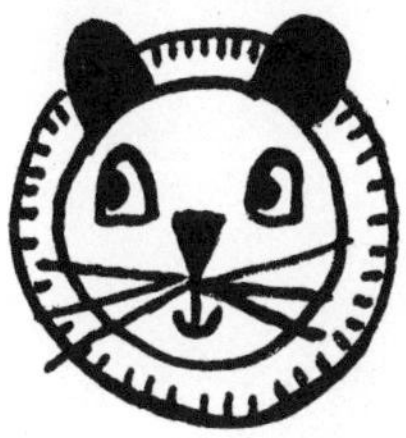

- 6" paper plate (dessert size)
- orange tempera paint
- brown and black construction paper
- paintbrushes
- felt-tipped markers, glue, scissors

Directions

Day One— Paint paper plates orange. Let dry.
Day Two— Fringe edges of paper plate to form lion's mane. Cut ears from brown paper, and glue to the top of head. Make eyes, nose, and mouth with cut paper or markers. Cut thin black strips for whiskers, and glue below rectangles of black paper.

Curly Lamb

Materials

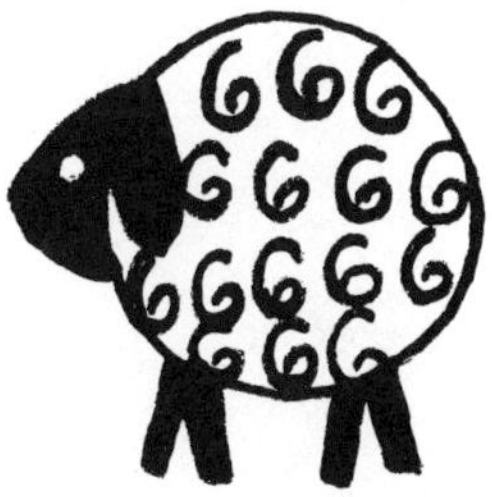

- 6" paper plate
- sixteen 1" x 4" strips of white paper
- 3 1/2"-base triangle of black construction paper for nose
- black paper scraps for feet and ear
- white paper scraps for eye
- fat pencil, scissors, glue

Directions

Cut to round off one point of the black triangle nose. Glue this to paper plate. Curl, using fat pencil, all 16 strips of white paper, and glue these curls all over plate. Cut eye from white paper and triangle ear from black paper, and glue in place. Ear may be folded over so that it stands out.

St. Patrick's Day Painting

Concept

The value of a color can be changed by adding white. (This painting lesson can be introduced with a discussion that explains the association of the color green with St. Patrick's Day.)

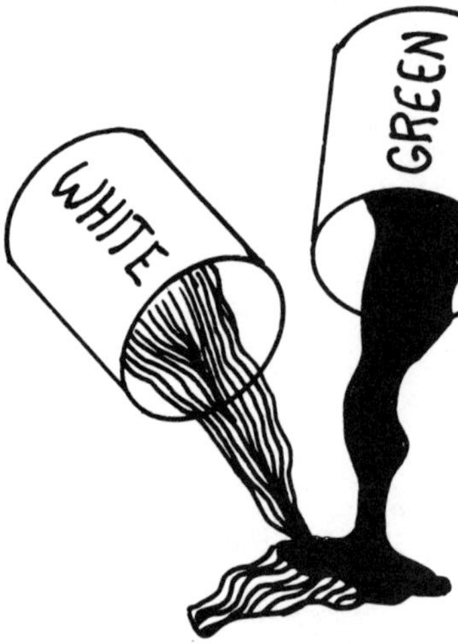

Materials (for younger children)

- container of green tempera
- container of white tempera
- 2 empty jars
- brushes, paper

Directions

Pour equal amounts of green paint into empty jars. Demonstrate the color change by adding a *small* amount of white paint to the first jar, and a *large* amount to the second. Mix and observe. Have the children then use the different shades of green for a St. Patrick's Day painting.

Materials (for older children)

- container of green tempera
- container of white tempera
- styrofoam meat trays for mixing (1 per child)
- brushes, water cans, paper

Directions

Demonstrate the changes in color produced by adding different amounts of white to the green paint. Let children mix their own shades of green in the meat tray and make a St. Patrick's Day painting.

String Wind Designs

Concept

Line can show movement.

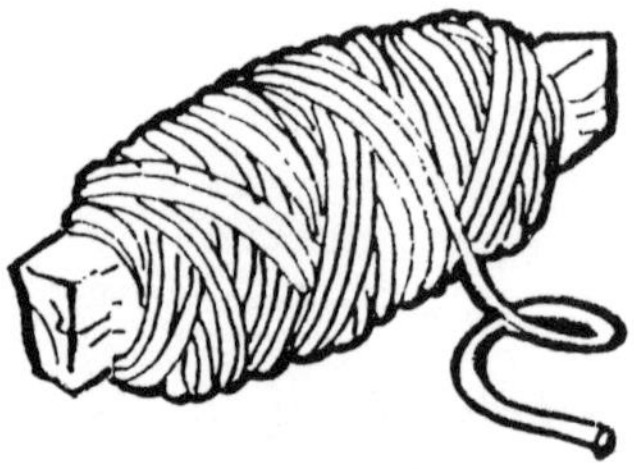

Materials

- 9" x 12" white drawing paper cut in half
- 18" string
- light blue tempera paint in each of several paint pans

Directions

Soak the string in paint, leaving a 4" or 5" section to hold. Place soaked string in a wriggly fashion on a half piece of paper. Lay second half-sheet on top. Place one hand firmly on top of paper. Pull string with free hand along all edges of paper. There will be a design on both of the sheets of paper.

Circus Train (good for kindergarten)

Motivation: Discuss the kinds of animals we see at the circus. Have each child pretend to be one particular animal. Ask him/her to think about the way in which that animal moves. Does it move quickly and quietly? Does it tromp or trot? Does it hop or jump about? Play a record with march or circus music on it. Have the children move around the room as the animal they have chosen, in time to the music. Then have them sit down and tell what their animal looks like—color, size, shape, etc.

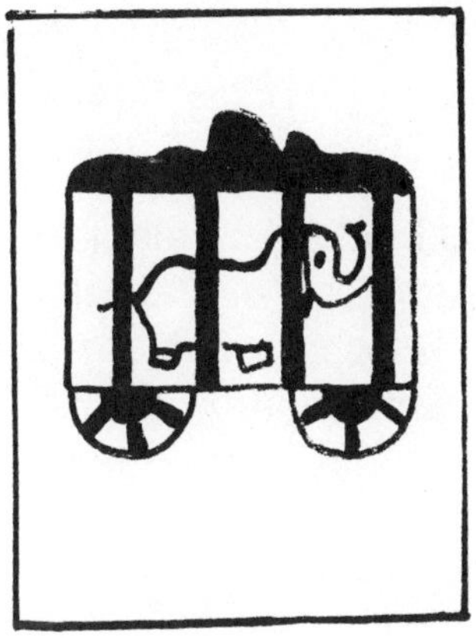

Materials

- tempera paint, brushes
- 12" x 18" manila paper
- four 1" black strips of construction paper
- paper scrap box or wallpaper samples
- glue, scissors

Directions

Day One —Have children paint their animals on manila paper. If it is not possible to work with the entire class, work with small groups or with individuals at the easel. Let dry.

Day Two—Glue the four black strips on top of the painting to form a cage. Then cut wheels and decorate tops of cages using scraps from the scrap box. The separate cars can be joined together to form a circus train for a room decoration.

Paper Plate Elephants

Concept

Circle shapes can be used to make animals.

Elephant Head (for younger children)

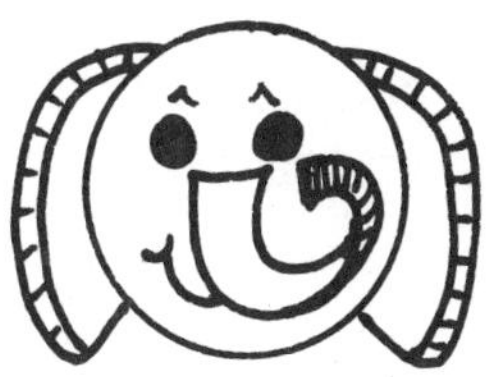

Materials

- two 9" paper plates per child
- 3" x 9" strip of colored paper
- gray tempera
- black paint or markers
- glue, brushes

Directions

Paint the two paper plates gray. Let dry. Cut one plate in half for ears. Glue ears to right and left sides of the second plate. Curl paper strip trunk and glue to middle of head. Add eyes and mouth with black paint or markers.

Moveable Circus Elephant (for older children)

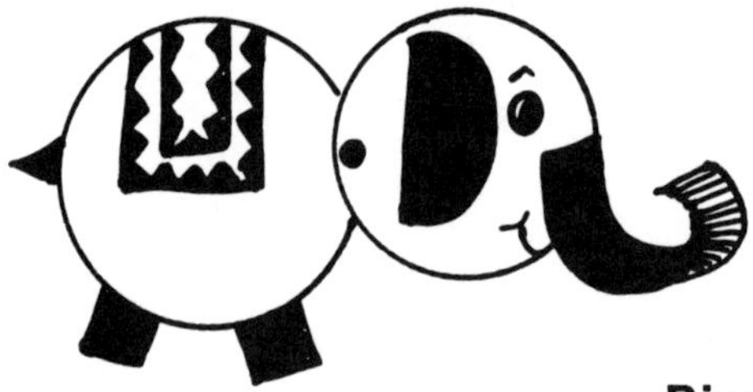

Materials

- one 9" paper plate (body)
- one 6" paper plate (head)
- one paper fastener
- gray tempera
- 2" x 9" strip of colored paper for trunk
- paper and fabric scraps
- black marker
- brushes, glue, scissors

Directions

Paint the two plates gray. Let dry. Attach head to body with paper fastener. Curl strip and attach to back of small plate for trunk. Cut and glue two rectangles for feet, one small triangle tail, and one half circle for ear. Add eye with marker, and make decorative blanket with paper or fabric scraps, yarn, rick-rack, etc.

Circus Clown

Concept

Shapes can be combined to form a head.

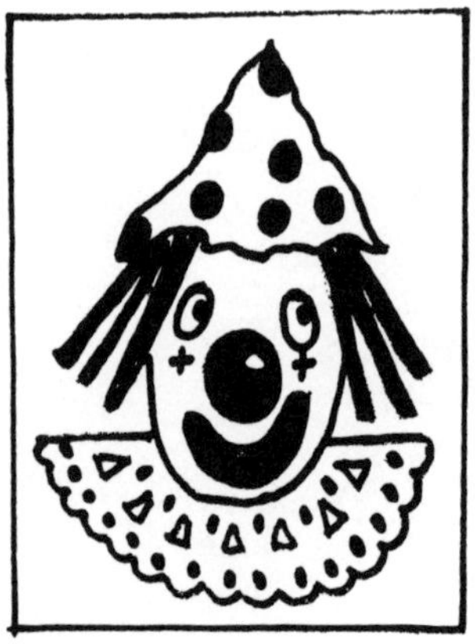

Materials

- 9" x 12" black construction paper for background
- 6" (high) pink oval
- half of a 6" paper doily
- yellow construction paper
- red or orange yarn for hair
- crayons or felt-tipped markers
- glue

Directions

Glue pink oval to middle of black paper. Tear a triangle from yellow paper to form hat, and glue on head. Glue on yarn for hair. Glue half-doily to bottom of oval for ruffled collar. Using crayons or markers, add facial features. Decorate hat with polka-dots.

Motivation: Bring in several pictures of clowns. Discuss the shapes that combine to make a clown's face. Using the flannel board, have children combine shapes such as ovals, triangles, and circles to form a clown's face.

Accordion Clown (for older children)

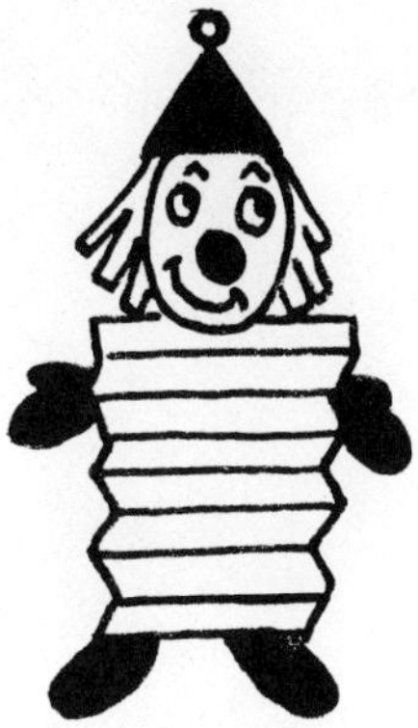

Materials
- 12" x 4 1/2" rectangle of red construction paper
- 4" x 5" oval of pink construction paper
- paper scrap box
- yarn
- glue, scissors

Directions
Fold red paper rectangle to make pleats. This will form the clown's body. Glue pink oval to top for head. Using paper scraps, cut out a triangle hat, clown hands, feet, and facial features and hair. Glue these to body and head of clown. Attach yarn at top to make clown jump.

Clown Collage

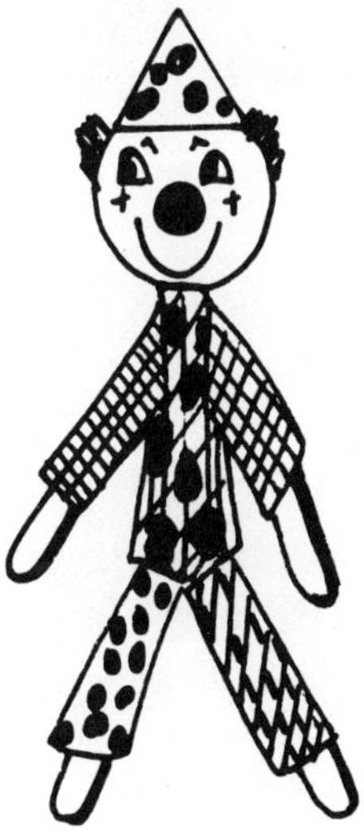

Concept
A variety of materials can be overlapped.

Materials
- 9" x 12" background paper
- 5 wooden craft sticks per child
- 3" pink construction paper circle
- paper and small precut fabric scraps
- buttons, yarn, crumpled tissue, beans, etc.
- glue, scissors

Directions
Glue pink circle near top of background paper. Glue craft sticks to form body. Dress clown with fabric scraps. Add face details with buttons and/or other items listed above. Cut out paper triangle for hat and glue to head.

Butterfly Magic

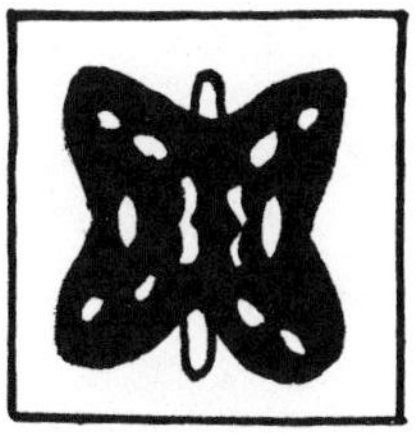

Materials
- 9" x 12" black construction paper
- glitter
- scissors, glue

Directions
Either precut butterfly shapes from black paper or have children cut on the fold to form the shape. Draw various designs on butterflies with glue, and cover with glitter.

3-D Birds

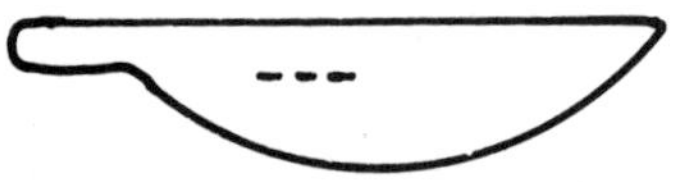

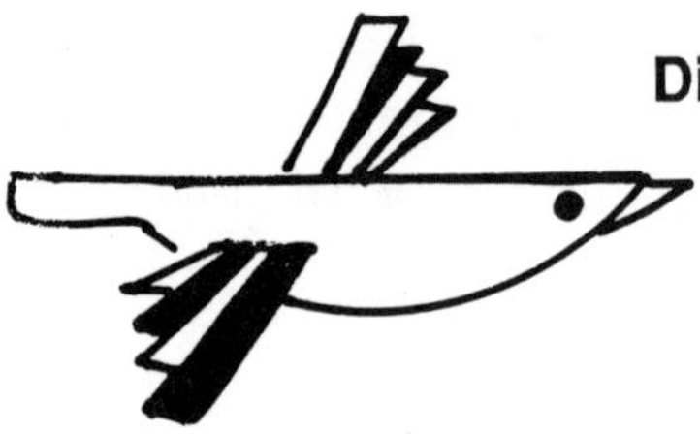

Concept

Paper can be folded to make a three-dimensional shape.

Materials:

- 9" x 12" construction paper
- 6" x 9" construction paper (different color)
- small triangle beak
- scissors

Directions

Fold 9" x 12" paper in half. Place pattern (as shown in first drawing on left) on the fold, trace, and cut. Fold wings from 6" x 9" paper back and forth like an accordion. Cut a slit in the body of the bird. Insert wings. Add eyes with marker, and glue on triangle beak. Spread body halves slightly so that bird will sit.

Optional

A nest for your bird to perch upon can be made from twigs glued to a coffee can lid.

Paper Sculpture Techniques

Paper sculpture creates a three-dimensional effect when using techniques such as cutting, folding, curling, pleating, fringing, rolling, and twisting. The variety of projects presented here utilizes some form of paper sculpture, although many creative ways for using paper will be suggested by the materials themselves once the work is begun. It is a good idea for the teacher to demonstrate each of the methods to acquaint the children with the process and to stimulate their thinking. Select only a few of these techniques to demonstrate at one time. The following basic forms can be taught.

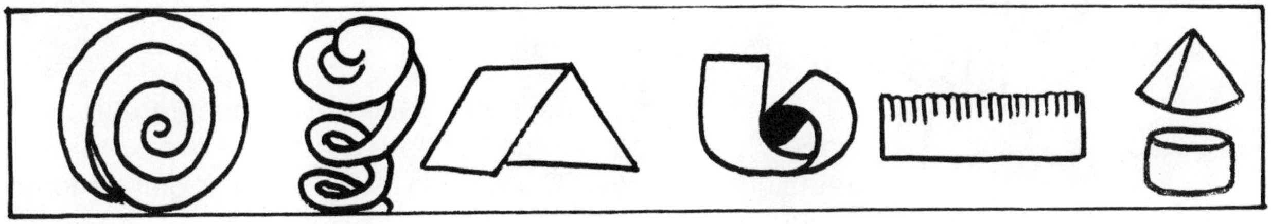

- Make a spiral by cutting into the edge of a circle and following around and around toward the center.

- Fold a rectangular piece of paper in half. This may suggest possibilities such as a tent or roof.

- Make a curl by tightly wrapping a paper strip around a fat pencil or by pulling a paper strip between the thumb and the edge of *closed* scissor blades held firmly in the hand.

- To pleat, fold a rectangular piece of paper back and forth several times.

- Make even snips along the edge of paper to make a fringe for grass, hair, eyelashes, etc.

- Roll a rectangular piece of paper and staple or glue overlapping edges to form a cylinder for use as a tree trunk, leg, drum, and the like. A cone shape can be made by cutting from the edge to the center of a circle and overlapping the cut edges to form a teepee or witch's hat.

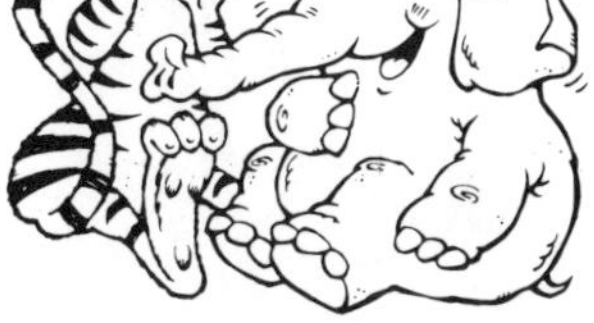

Chatter Box

Too often there is little time to precut materials. Buttons, seeds, and crumpled tissue make good eyes, noses, and mouths. Faces can be printed with empty spools.

APRIL IDEAS

April Showers

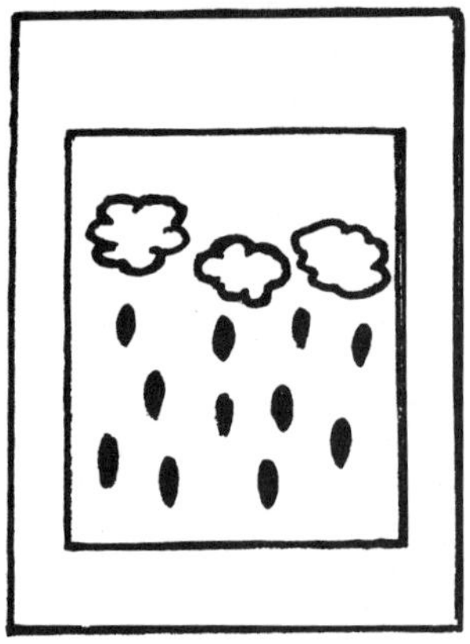

Concept

Texture can be found in nature.

Materials

- 9" x 12" blue construction paper
- cotton balls or raw cotton
- seeds or small beans
- glue

Directions

Shape cotton balls into puffy clouds. Glue near top of paper. Place dots of glue beneath clouds, all over remainder of paper. Put a seed on each dot of glue to form raindrops.

Forsythia in Bloom

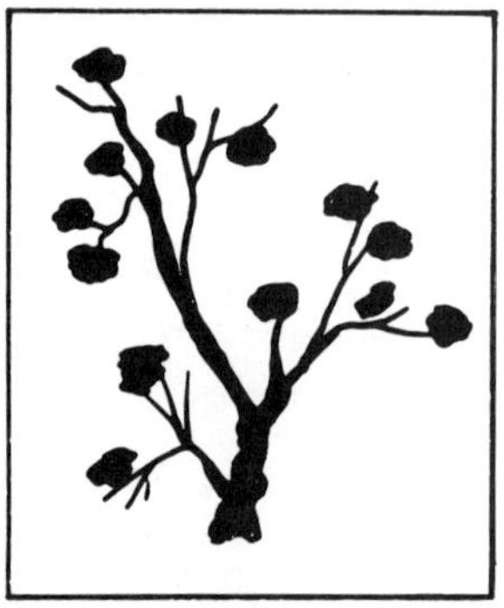

Materials

- thin black tempera paint
- drinking straw
- 9" x 12" construction paper for background
- yellow and green tissue squares
- glue

Directions

Drop about 1 tsp. of black tempera near the bottom of background paper. With head at table level, immediately begin blowing paint, using straw, toward the top of the paper to form a branchlike pattern. Paper can be turned to vary the direction of paint. (***Caution*** **:** remind children ***not*** to inhale, just to blow.) When dry, add crumpled tissue to form forsythia blossoms and leaves

Motivation: This poem can be used as motivation or follow-up for the next activity.

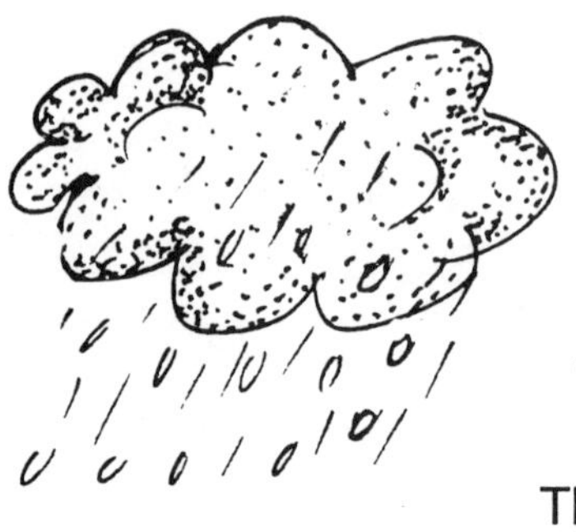

Plip, plop, drip, drop
The rain begins to patter.
Plip, plop, drip, drop
Watch the raindrops spatter.

Plip, plop, drip, drop
The puddles are shiny and round.
Plip, plop, drip, drop
They're scattered all over the ground.

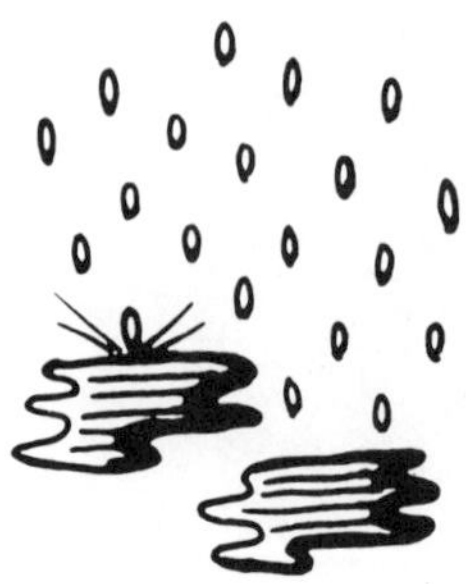

Shiny Puddles

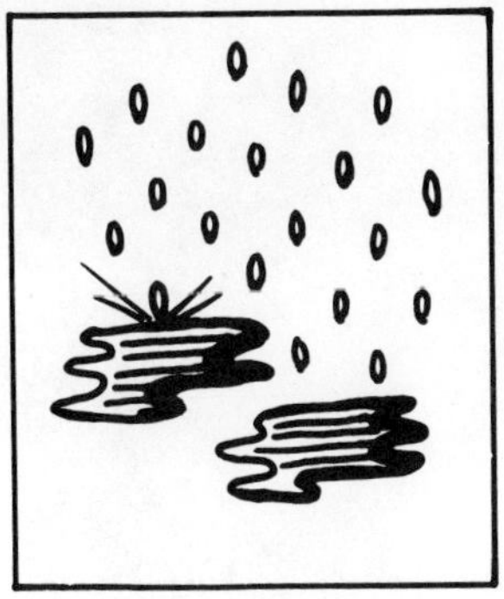

Materials
- 9" x 12" blue construction paper
- aluminum foil
- glitter
- glue, scissors

Directions

Ask child to cut a free-form shape from foil. Glue to background paper, shiny side up, for puddle. Dot paper with glue. Sprinkle with glitter and shake gently.

Pastel Painting

Concept

Two colors can be mixed to form a third color.

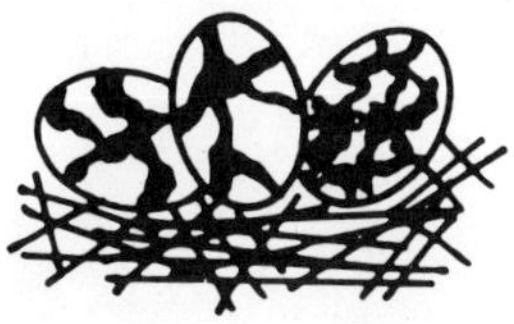

Materials
- blue and white fingerpaint
- fingerpaint paper

Directions

Place 1 tbls. of each color of fingerpaint on paper. Fingerpaint a design combining colors. Let dry.

Extension

Finished painting can be cut into several egg shapes and glued to a piece of background paper. Pieces of uncooked spaghetti can be glued underneath eggs for nest.

Pastel Easter Egg

Materials
- colored chalk
- plastic knife, scissors, or a vegetable scraper
- cookie pan (with sides)
- water
- precut white paper oval

Directions

Fill cookie pan with water. Have children scrape chalk shavings into water. Carefully lay white paper oval on surface of water (do not submerge). Lift off gently for a colorful egg. The floating chalk adheres to paper for a marbleized effect.

Hatching Chick

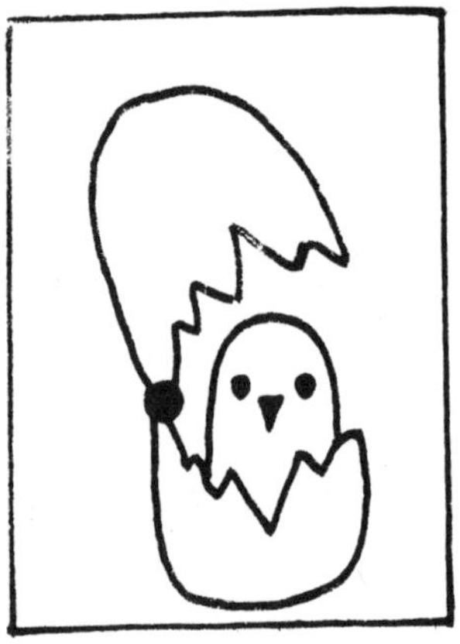

Concept

Shapes can be put together so that they move.

Materials

- 1 large orange oval of construction paper
- 1 small yellow oval of construction paper
- 1 paper fastener
- felt-tipped markers
- scissors, glue

Directions

Cut large oval in half using zig-zag lines. Attach egg sections together on left-hand side with paper fastener. Glue yellow oval to back of bottom half of orange egg. Add a triangle beak and two eyes with markers.

The Chicken Coop

Concept

Form can be three-dimensional. (This activity can be used as motivation for a visit to a farm.)

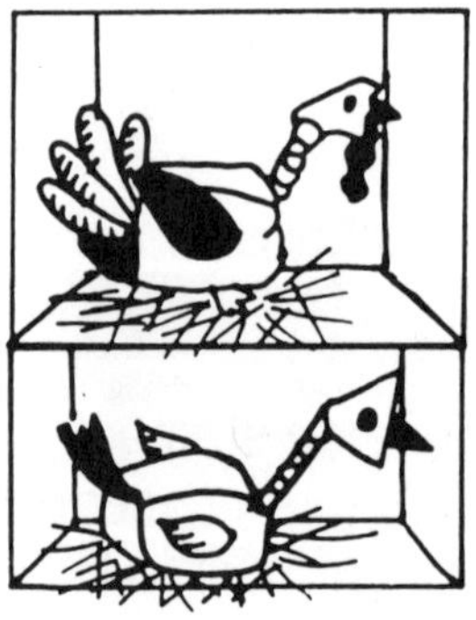

Materials

- brown lunch bag
- newspaper
- paper scrap box
- straw
- box (shoe box or bigger)
- glue, scissors

Directions

Stuff bag half-full of crumpled newspaper. Twist top half of bag to form neck and head. Add wings, tail feathers, and wattles out of construction paper scraps and glue into place. Turn box on its side. Line bottom with straw glued into place. Put chicken inside box. Stack boxes together to form a coop.

Humpty Dumpty

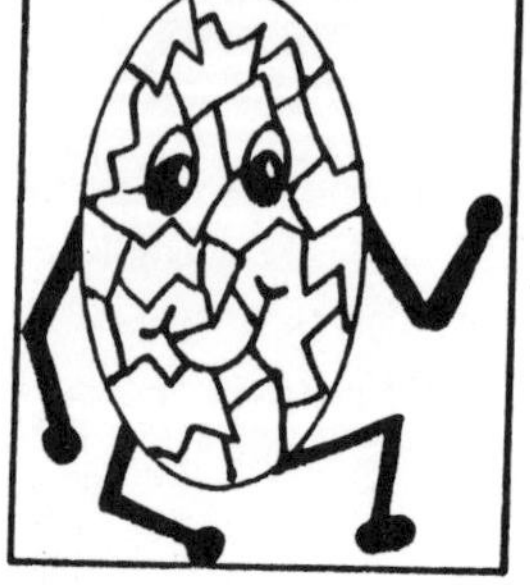

Materials

- crushed egg shells (clean and dry)
- shirt box lids
- 9" x 12" construction paper for background
- precut cardboard egg pattern
- black tissue
- glue
- markers

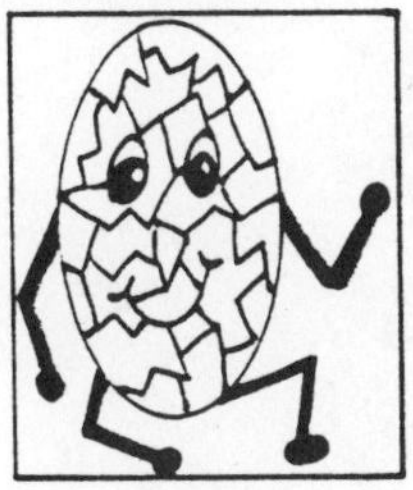

Directions

Trace egg pattern with marker onto background paper (teacher should do this for younger children). Cover this area with glue. Sprinkle egg shells on top. Shake excess shells gently over box lids. Add crushed tissue-paper eyes. Arms, legs, and mouth can be added with markers if desired.

Colorful Curly Caterpillars

Concept

Paper can be sculpted to form a three-dimensional object from nature. This is a good math lesson, too. Count to four, and make four rings.

Materials

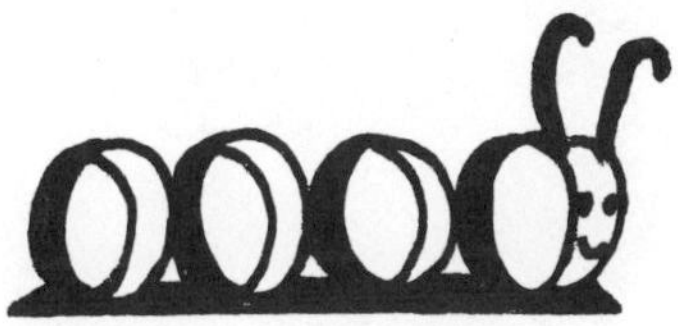

- 9" x 2" strips of various-colored construction paper (5 strips per child)
- 1/4" x 4" strips of paper for antennae (2 per child)
- felt-tipped markers
- scissors, glue

Directions

Use four of the 9" x 2" strips to form rings. Glue each one. Then glue these rings along the top of the remaining strip. Curl the two smaller strips for antennae and glue these to the top of the first ring. Add a face to this ring with markers.

Motivation: The following poem can be used in connection with the next three projects. The three bunnies mentioned in the poem can be cut out of white felt and used on the flannel board while presenting the poem.

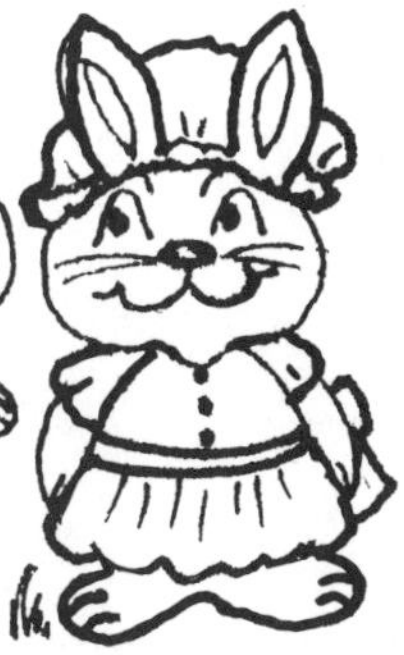

Three Hopping Bunnies

Three little bunnies so soft and furry
One hopped away in a great big hurry
Two little bunnies pink and white
Another hopped away and out of sight
One little bunny sitting all alone
He hopped away to his rabbit-hole home
No more bunnies, as you can see
They all hopped away—one, two, three.

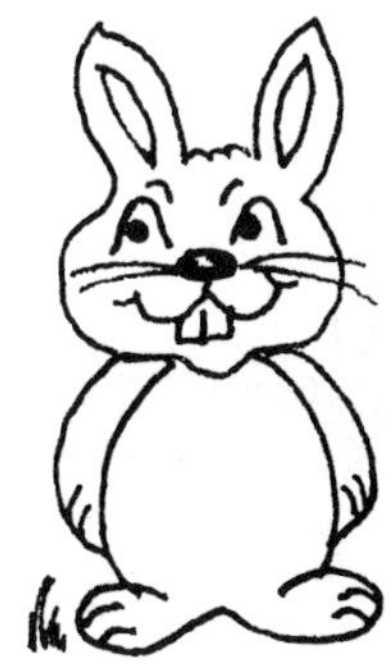

Paper Bag Bunny

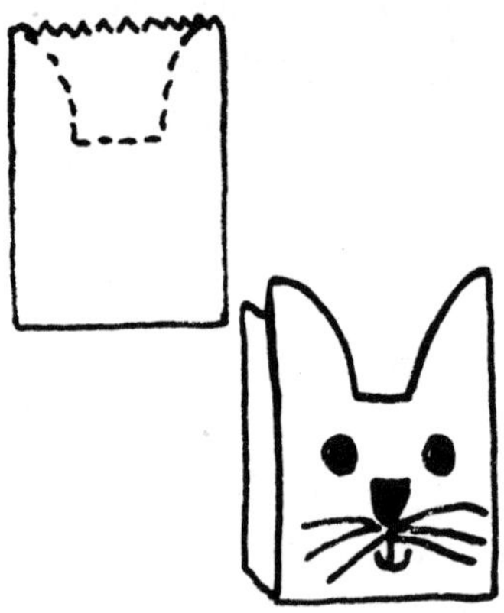

Materials
- white or brown lunch-sized paper bags
- tissue or construction paper scraps
- Easter grass
- scissors, glue

Directions

Leaving paper bag folded flat, cut along dotted lines as shown in diagram (teacher can cut for very young children). Using paper scraps, cut out black eyes and whiskers and pink nose and glue to front of bag. Open bag and fill with Easter basket grass. Fill with Easter treats.

Honey Bun-ny

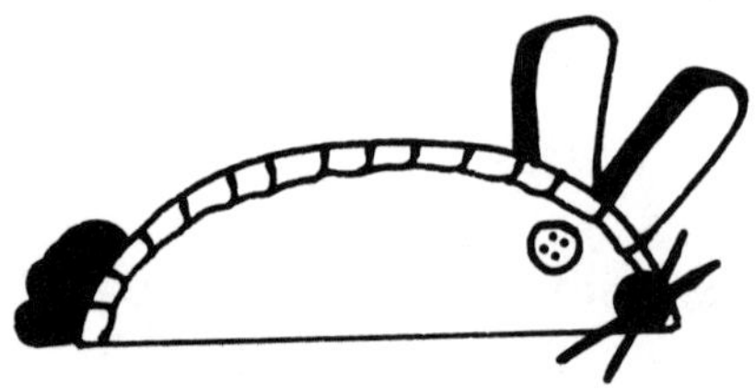

Materials
- half of a 9" paper plate
- two 1 1/2" x 9" pink paper strips
- cotton ball
- felt circle for nose (or pink crumpled tissue, pink pom-porn, pink cotton ball)
- dark button for eye
- black strips for whiskers
- glue

Directions

Fold each pink strip in half and glue to back of paper plate for ears. Glue whiskers in place and glue nose on top. Add eye and cotton-ball tail.

Bunny Basket

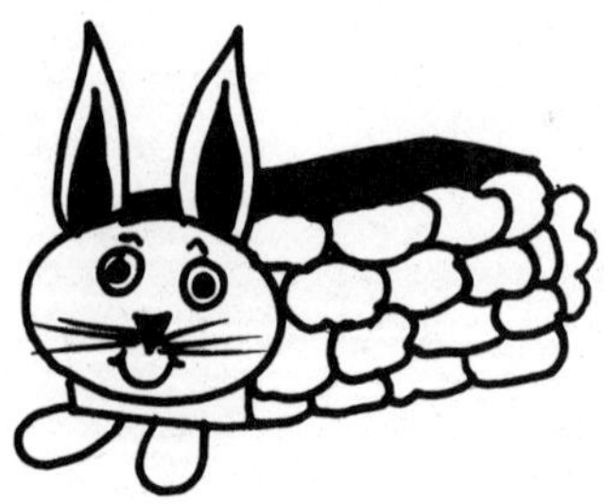

Materials
- small (8 oz.) juice or milk carton
- white paper
- cotton balls
- pink tissue
- black paper strips
- glue, scissors

Directions

Cut top off carton. On one end, glue white paper circle for head. Cut and glue white ears and feet. Use pink crumpled tissue for eyes and nose. Glue black whiskers in place. On remaining three sides, glue cotton balls. Fill with Easter grass and treats.

Learning about Line

Lines can show action, rhythm, and direction and can be combined to form patterns. Observe and identify the following types of lines found in the classroom: vertical, horizontal, diagonal, and curved; wavy, zig-zag, and broken lines; thick/thin lines, long/short lines, and light/dark lines. Vertical and horizontal lines can easily be recognized in architecture. All types of line can be found in the paintings of famous artists. For example, Edouard Manet's *Gare Saint-L'Azare*, Vincent Van Gogh's *Olive Grove*, Joseph Stella's *The Brooklyn Bridge: Variations on a Theme*, Henri Rousseau's *The Jungle: Monkeys and Oranges.* Many of the works by Piet Mondrian, Henri Matisse, and Pablo Picasso are excellent to use in the study of line. Inexpensive prints are available at museums and some bookstores or, you'll find them in art books at your local library.

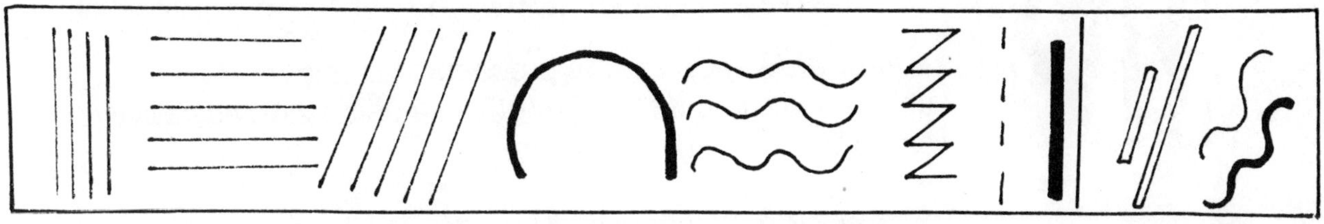

Line Activities—Here are some possible methods for teaching *line.*

1. Using the flannel board, have children use a piece of yarn to show one kind of line. Each child must name the line shown. Remind the children not to close the ends of their lines or a *shape* will be formed.

2. Give each child an 18" piece of string to represent a line. Allow time to stretch, wiggle, and turn it to see how many different types of lines can be duplicated.

3. To prepare the children for drawing to music, play a record with contrasting rhythms. Ask them to pretend to be conductors, waving their arms in time to the music. The children will enjoy this combination of movement and music.

4. Using chalk and large sheets of paper, have children draw to music while sitting on the floor.

5. Form a line with your class. Move in and around the tables to show a wavy line. Stand at attention in a straight line. Have the class hold hands and form a zig-zag line. Or, play Simon Says using all the different lines.

6. Pass out several pieces of pipe cleaner and let the children bend and twist their own lines. Connect all the examples to form a large line sculpture.

MAY IDEAS

Line Art

Concept

Lines can make designs and patterns.

Materials

- 2" x 9" black construction paper strips
- glue
- scissors

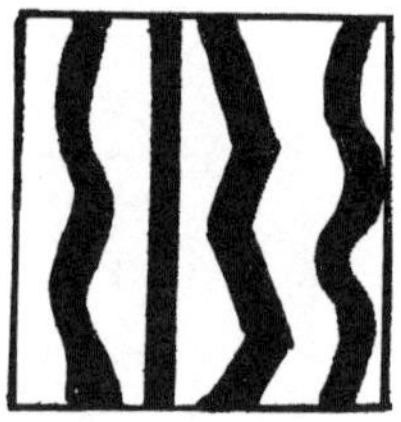

3 year olds —Put black paper strips on table. Have children cut these 2" strips lengthwise to make different widths. Glue to background paper leaving white spaces between the lines.

4 year olds —Use same procedure as above. However, children are to cut strips lengthwise using zig-zag, wavy, or straight lines. Glue as above.

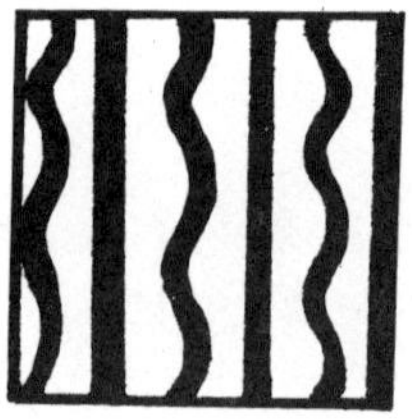

5 year olds —Use same procedure as for 4 year olds. Take this one step further by discussing how to form patterns using repetition of various lines. Have children place cut strips on paper first to create a *pattern.* When a pattern is achieved, glue strips to paper.

Hint

Two identical strips are formed when cutting the 2" strip lengthwise. Simply flip one over for a perfect match. Don't strive for or expect perfectly cut strips.

3-D Line Sculpture

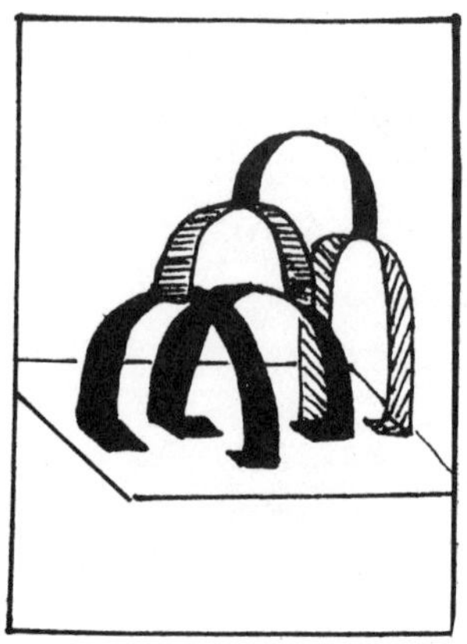

Concept

Lines can be used in a stand-up design.

Materials

- heavy paper or cardboard for base
- precut construction paper strips of various colors and sizes
- glue or paste

Directions

Fold strips 1/2" from each end. Apply glue on folded ends, and secure one end to base paper. Form an arch and fasten down the other end. The strips can be attached to one another, be positioned independently, or be overlapped.

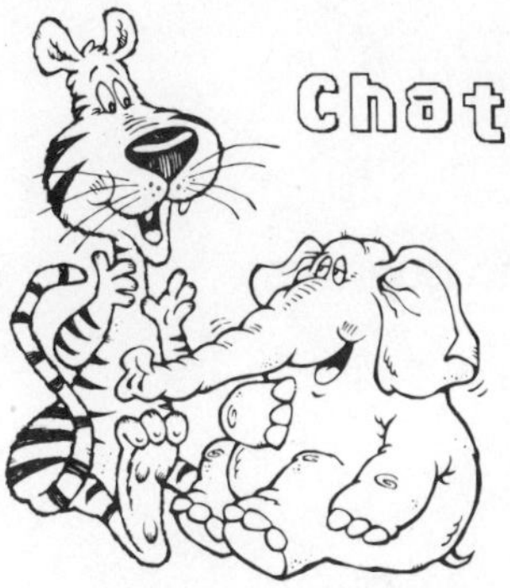

Chatter Box

Children need to feel good about their work without continual adult approval. It is not necessary to make comments each time a child does something. It is important to remain silent sometimes and allow children to work on their own.

Silly Shapes

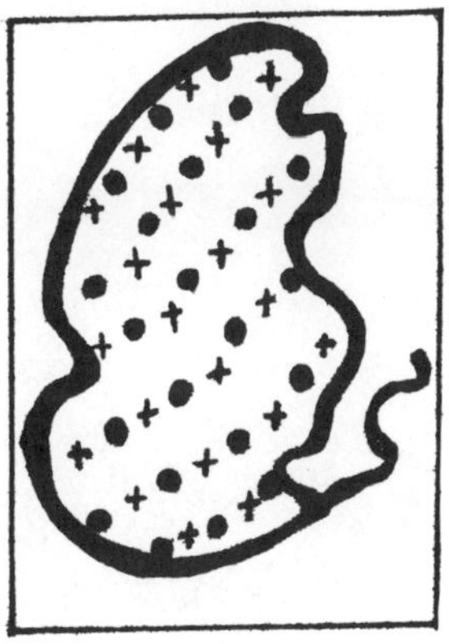

Concept

Lines can be closed to form a shape.

Materials

- 9" x 12" manila paper for background
- assorted wallpaper samples
- dark-colored yarn (the thicker the better)
- glue
- scissors

Directions

Cut wallpaper sample into any "silly" shape (large enough to almost fill the background paper). Put glue on back of shape, and glue to manila paper. Outline this shape with glue. Press the yarn around the shape to define and outline. Trim any excess yarn.

Creative Expressions

Motivation: The mirror is an ideal tool to use when learning about facial expressions. Look into a mirror and make a face that is happy, sad, scared, tired, angry, or surprised. Expressive faces cut from magazines will help in this discussion.

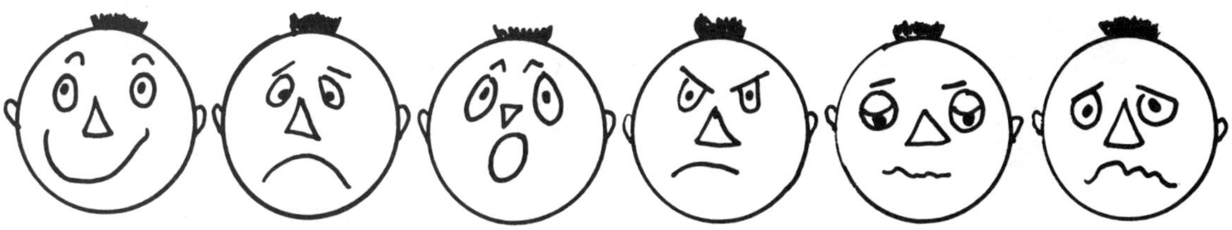

Creative Expressions

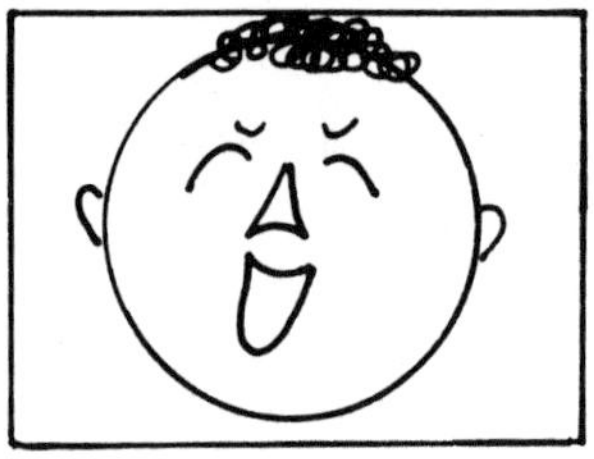

Concept

Lines and shapes can show expressions.

Materials

- 9" x 12" drawing paper (prefolded into quarters)
- felt markers
- 3 1/2" circle pattern (a jar lid is good)
- mirror

Directions

Trace a circle inside each of the folded sections of the paper. Draw a face on each circle to show a different feeling.

Caterpillar on Me!

***Motivation*:** Discuss the life cycle of the caterpillar (butterfly) with the children. Use the following poem as motivation and/or follow-up for the next activity.

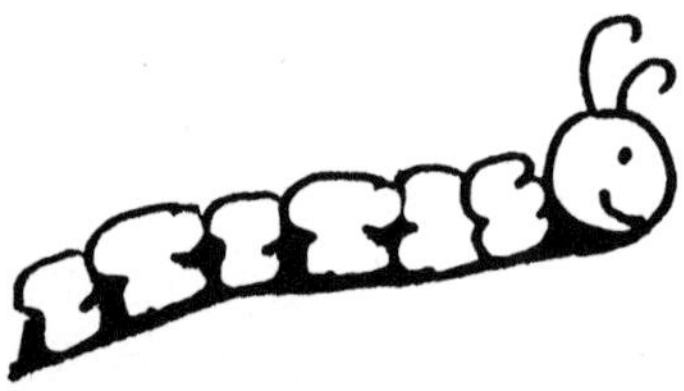

The Caterpillar

OOoh there's a caterpillar
Crawling up my arm
But it's okay
'Cause he means no harm.

He's up to my shoulder
And under my chin
I'll close my mouth
So he can't crawl in!

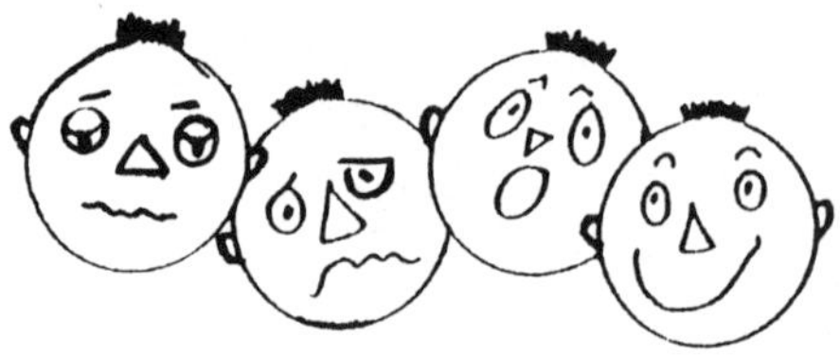

Materials

- 1" x 6" strip of colored construction paper
- scrap paper
- a variety of colored cotton balls
- masking tape
- felt markers
- glue, scissors

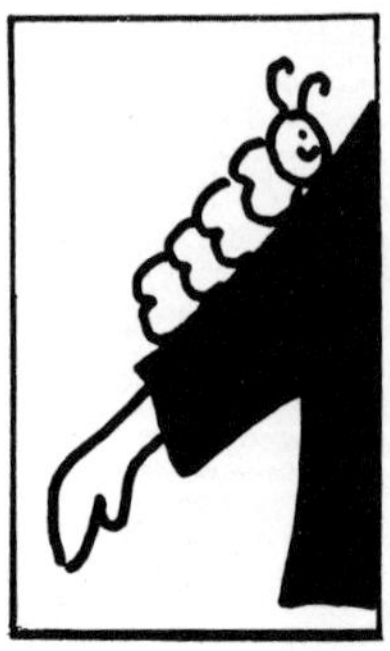

Directions

Cut head (about 2" circle) from scrap paper. Add face with markers. Fold bottom of head and glue to one end of paper strip. Cut two antennae and attach to head. Glue cotton balls (precolored or colored by shaking balls in a bag with a tiny amount of powdered tempera) along paper strip. Rolled masking tape can be placed on the underside of the caterpillar so it can be worn by the child.

Motivation: The following poem can be used as motivation or follow-up for the next project.

Mother Robin

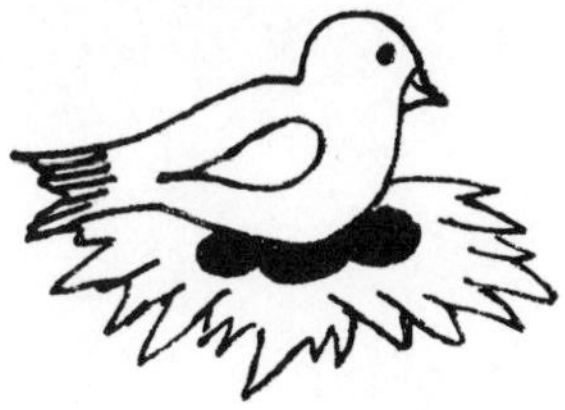

Mother robin built a nest
High up in a tree
She padded it with straw and twigs
And made it hard to see.

One spring day she laid her eggs
A pretty blue were they
She sat upon them till they hatched
And helped them fly away.

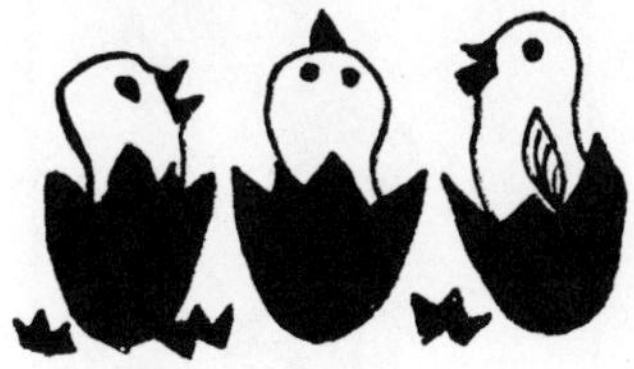

Robin's Nest

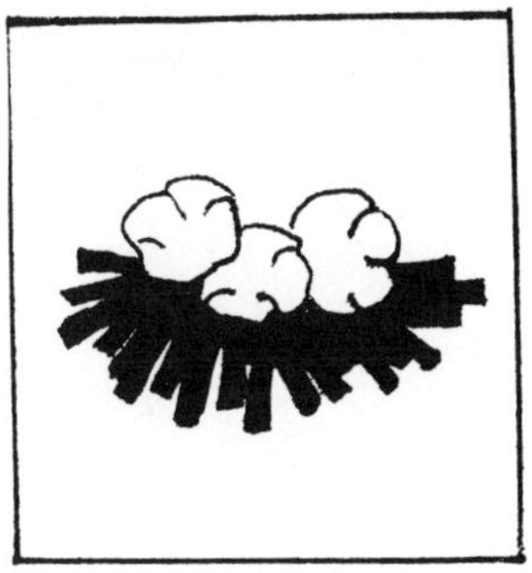

Materials

- any shallow lid
- 9" x 4" piece of brown construction paper
- 3 blue cotton balls
- glue
- scissors

Directions

Cut the entire brown rectangle width-wise into thin strips. Overlapping strips, randomly glue to lid to form nest. Glue three blue cotton balls in center of nest to represent a robin's eggs. (Cotton balls can be colored by shaking them in a bag with a small amount of powdered tempera.)

May Flowers

Concept

Shapes can be repeated to form objects in nature.

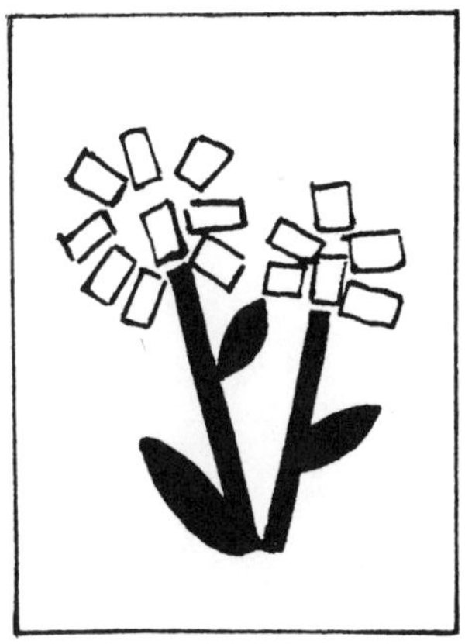

Materials

- 9" x 12" piece of spring-colored construction paper for background
- green construction paper
- sponges
- tempera paint
- glue, scissors

Directions

Cut or tear green paper to form two stems and several leaves. Glue to background paper. Using an "up-down" motion, spongepaint petals on top of stems.

Thumbprint Blossoms

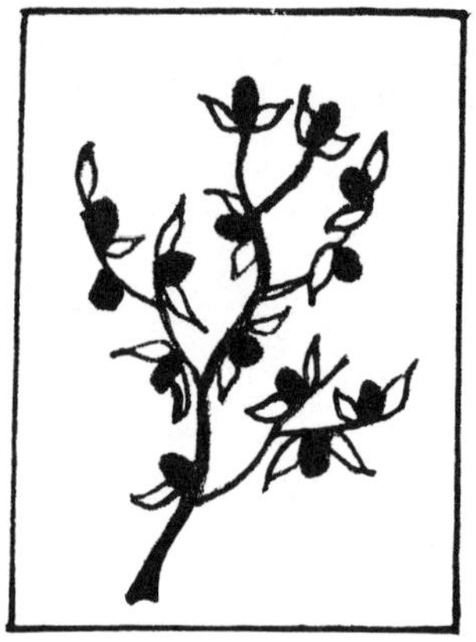

Materials
- white drawing paper
- brown or black felt-tipped markers
- various colors of tempera paint
- styrofoam meat trays
- paper towels

Directions

Place a folded paper towel in the bottom of a meat tray. Pour small amount of *thick* tempera paint in tray. Draw a branch on white paper with brown marker. Dip a finger in paint and print blossoms using a different fingerprint for each color. (Use only one color for younger children.) You can glue green crumpled tissue paper on for leaves.

Chalk Flowers

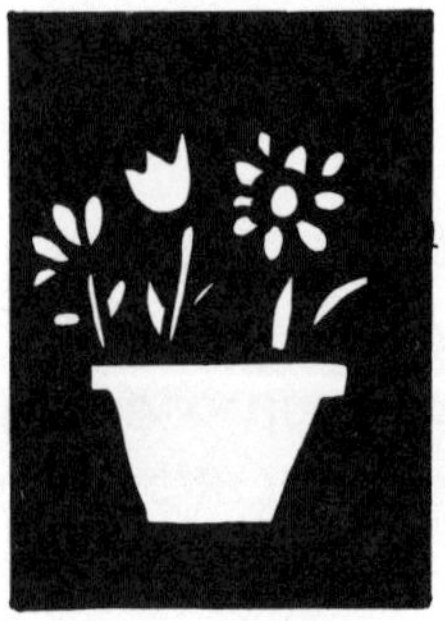

Concept

Colors are found in the things we see in spring.

Materials
- 9" x 12" black construction paper
- 4 1/2" cardboard flower pot pattern
- colored chalk
- scissors, glue, pencil

Directions

Trace and cut flower pot and glue near bottom of black paper. With colored chalk, add flowers by using sides and tip of chalk. Remind children to be careful not to smear. Finished drawings can be sprayed with fixative or hair spray.

Mother's Day Sachet

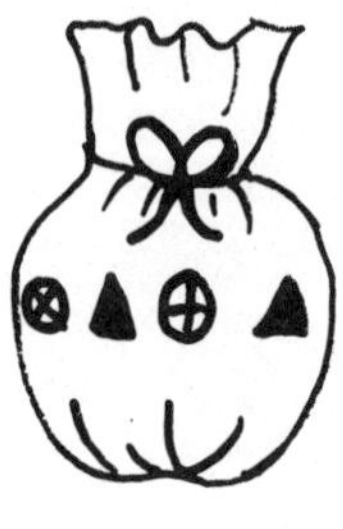

Materials
- 8" square of unbleached muslin (or any inexpensive fabric)
- tempera paint
- small printing gadgets (spools, lids, etc.)
- 12" ribbon or yarn
- potpourri or perfumed cotton balls

Directions

Using gadgets, print with tempera on fabric square. When dry, place potpourri or cotton balls in center of unprinted side. Gather and tie with ribbon.

Touch, Feel, and Create
(Teaching Texture)

Sandpaper, modeling clay, satin ribbons, buttons, seeds, felt, crumpled tissue, cotton balls— all are great tactile materials for teaching texture. In addition, processes such as fingerpainting, rubbings, and printing provide a means for teaching visual texture. Encourage the children to *touch* things, to describe how they feel; and to express themselves using the following activities.

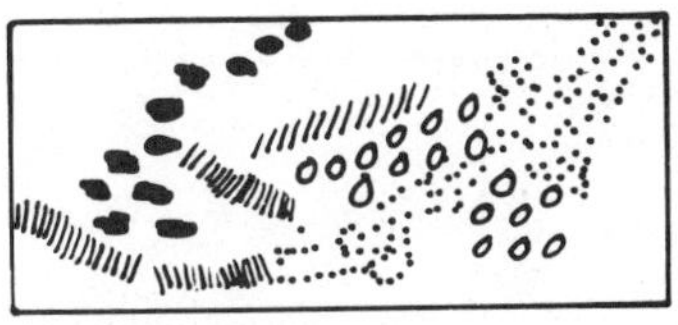

It's in the Bag

Fill several bags with a variety of rough, natural textures such as sand, fine birdseed, sawdust, raw sugar, or crushed eggshells. Draw a design in glue on cardboard. Choosing one texture at a time, sprinkle small quantity over paper. Shake excess into box lid. Repeat process with other textures.

Texture on a Shape

Distribute precut cardboard fish. Provide confetti, glitter, crumpled tissue, and foil or colored paper cut in very small pieces to be arranged and glued on fish. Glue fish collages to background paper or use for bulletin board display.

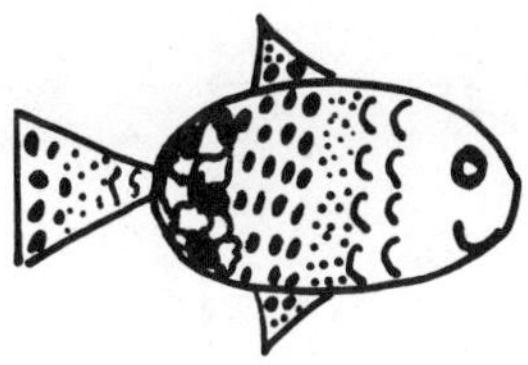

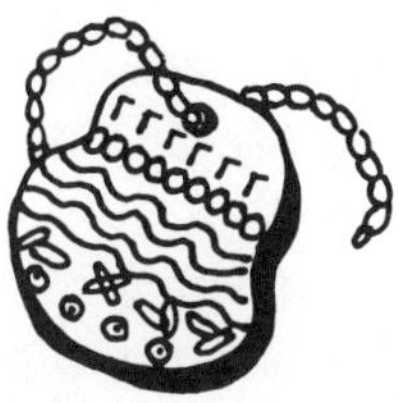

Press a Texture

Roll out a piece of clay (air-dry type or bakers clay). Create textures in clay by pressing small objects into the surface. Buttons, paper clips, spools, wooden craft sticks, spoons, forks, etc., may be used for imprinting.

Print a Texture

Glue heavy string or cord around a juice can. Let dry. Apply tempera paint with brush to string. Roll can across construction paper of a contrasting color. Re-apply paint and roll can in a different direction to form an interesting texture.

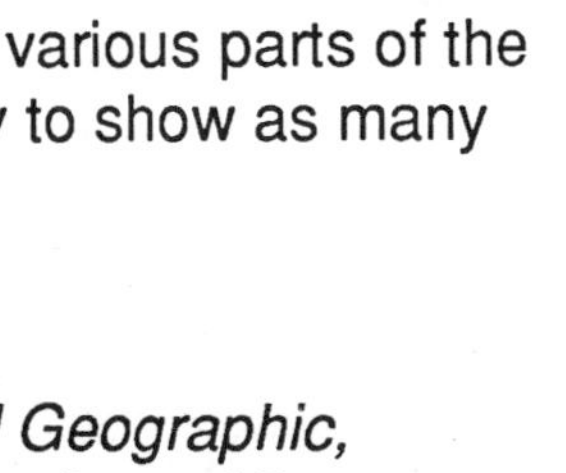

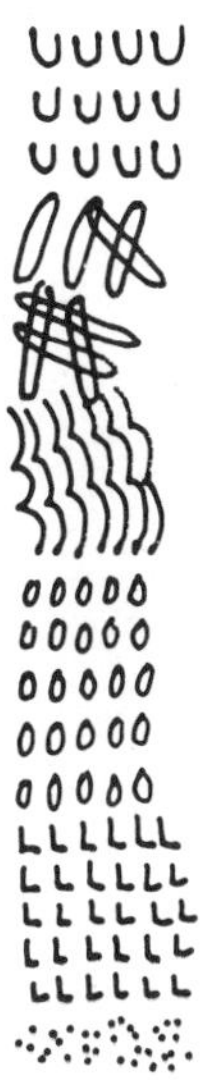

Fingerpaint a Texture

Create an undersea picture with fingerpaint. Use various parts of the hand to suggest sand, fish, plants, and rocks. Try to show as many different textures as possible.

Match a Texture

Choose a picture from the museum, the *National Geographic, Ranger Rick,* or *Life* magazine that shows at least three different textures. Gather samples of each pictured texture. Have the child face the picture with hands behind his/her back. Place one texture sample in child's hand, and ask him/her to identify it in the picture. Take turns with the rest of the class.

JUNE IDEAS

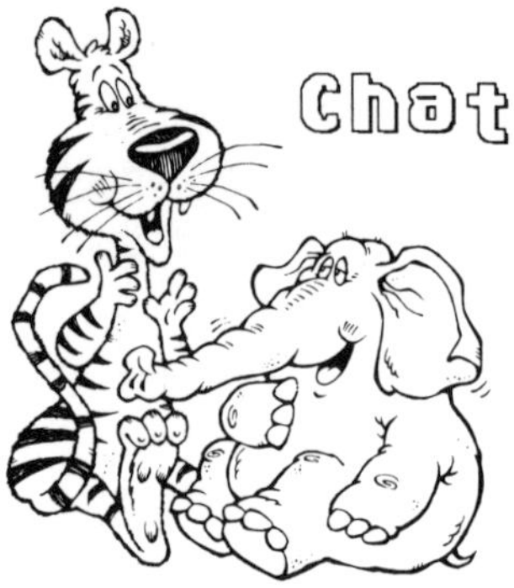

Chatter Box

Exposure to the appreciation of fine arts can begin in the preschool classroom. Display prints of famous works of art at child's eye level. These can be referred to from time to time in class discussions without formal instruction. This is a wonderful way to interrelate art with other classroom activities.

Giant Texture Puzzle

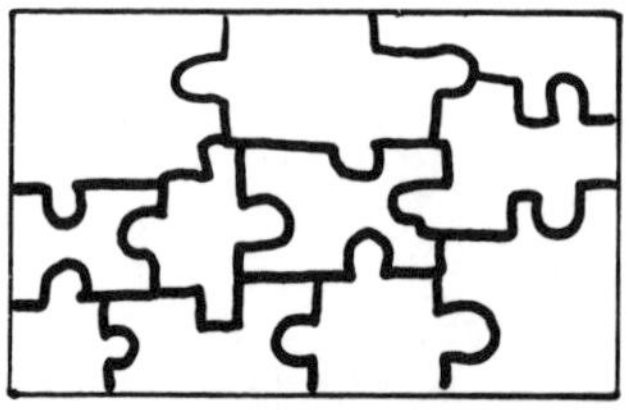

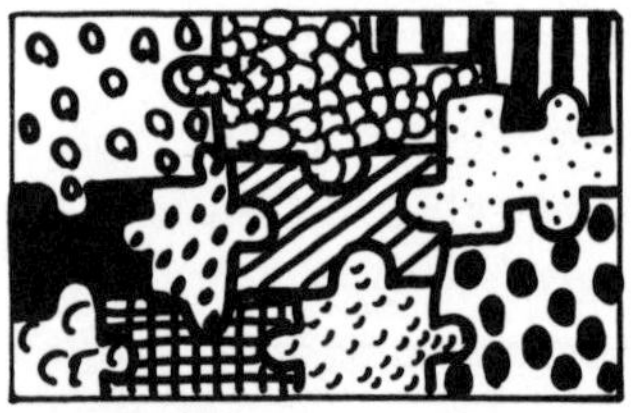

Concept

Textures can be seen.

Materials

- 22" x 28" piece of white poster board
- 3 colors of tempera paint
- paintbrushes, water

Directions

Demonstrate various ways to show texture with paint. This can be done by repeating or overlapping shapes and lines. The teacher should draw a puzzle (consisting of the same number of pieces as there are children) on poster board with marker. Show puzzle to class. Then cut into pieces and distribute. Have each child paint a textured design. Let dry and have fun trying to re-assemble the puzzle.

Sun Face

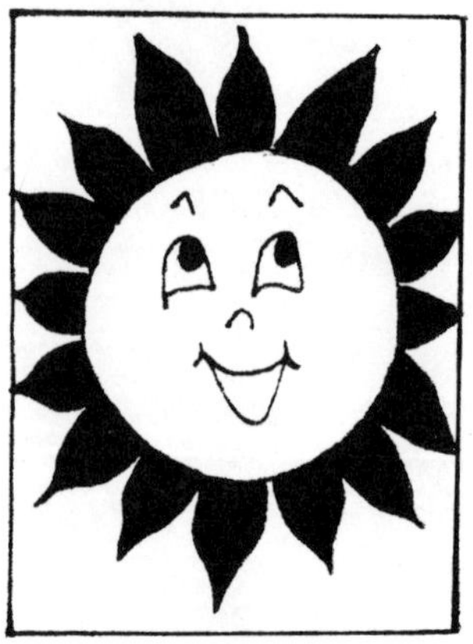

Materials

- 12" x 18" black or dark blue construction paper
- colored chalk: red, orange, yellow, black
- hair spray

Directions

Identify the colors found in the sun. Make a large chalk drawing beginning with a circle shape. Let children experiment with blending the various colors using a tissue or their fingers. When sun is completed, make a face using black chalk. Spray entire surface with hair spray.

Undersea World of (name of school)

Motivation: The following activities are all related to the undersea world. Transform your classroom into a sea environment by hanging blue and green streamers, fish, crabs, octopus, jellyfish, etc., from the ceiling. Arrange shells and other sea creatures around the room also. Story time, snacks, and learning centers could all be integrated into this theme.

Goldfish

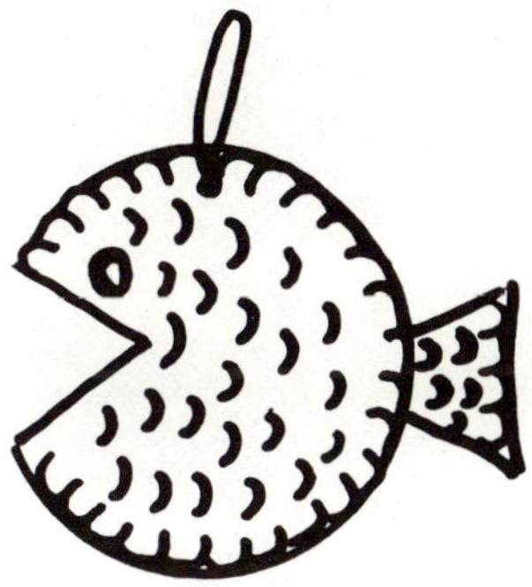

Concept

Shapes can be re-arranged to form a different shape.

Materials

- 9" paper plate
- orange tempera paint
- paper scrap box
- glue, scissors, brushes
- stapler, paper punch, string

Directions

Paint both sides of paper plate. When dry, cut a triangle from plate and staple to opposite end for tail. Triangle fins can be cut from scraps. Decorate body as desired. Punch hole in top and tie string for hanging.

Fish in a Pond

Motivation: Read *Swimmy* by Leo Lionni to the class and discuss how the illustrations were made.

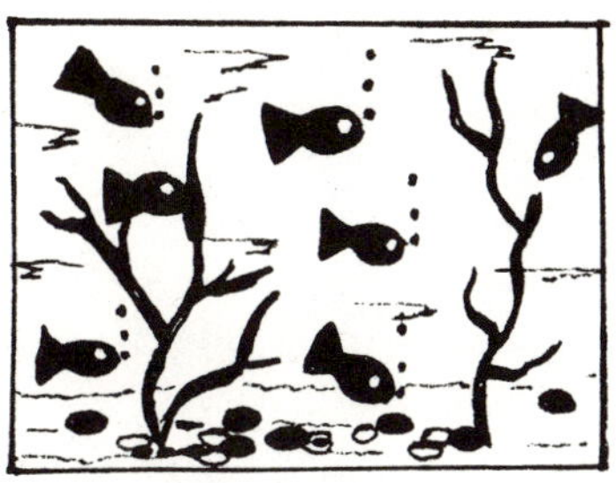

Materials

- blue and yellow fingerpaint
- fingerpaint paper
- precut sponge fish (glue on spool for handle)
- orange tempera
- black crayon or felt-tipped marker

Directions

Day One —Fingerpaint an underwater scene using and blending the two colors. Let dry.
Day Two —Sponge paint orange fish on top of underwater scene. Let dry. Eyes and mouth can be added with black crayon or marker.

Cylinder Fish

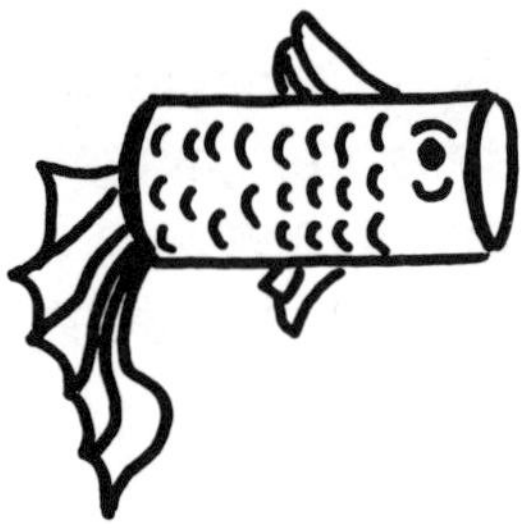

Materials

- paper or cardboard tube
- any color tempera paint or silver spray paint
- construction paper (for fins)
- tissue or crepe paper (for tail)
- colored felt markers, glitter, or foil/paper scraps
- glue, scissors, brushes
- paper punch, yarn

Directions

Paint or spray paint the tube. Let dry. Punch in tip and knot yarn for hanging. Add tail and fins as shown in the illustration.Decorate imaginatively with foil, glitter, paper scraps, or markers.

Jellyfish: Suspend half a white 9" paper plate from yarn. Glue on long white crepe paper or tissue-paper tentacles.

Octopus: Spongepaint both sides of a 9" paper plate gray. Curl eight 1" x 9" gray paper strips and glue around plate. Add two big black eyes, and hang with string.

Eel: Cut a 9" construction paper circle of any color into a spiral. Add eyes. Suspend from center with string.

Motivation: The following poem can be used as motivation and/or follow-up for the "Undersea World" activities.

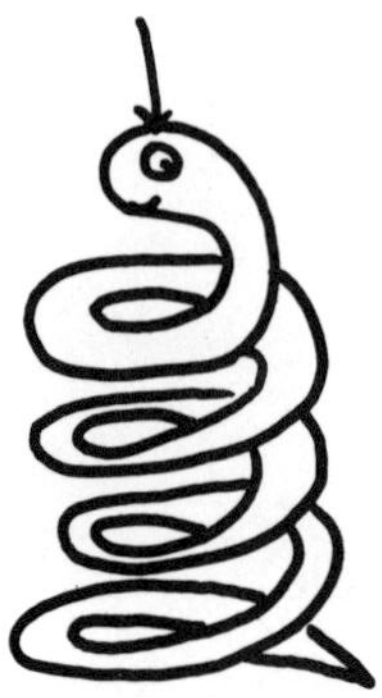

The SEA

Under the sea, way down deep
Fishes swim and red crabs creep.
The octopus slithers past the eel,
and jellyfish float to find a meal.

Under the sea, way down deep,
Shells and clams and oysters sleep.
The grasses wiggle to and fro,
Under the sea, way down below.

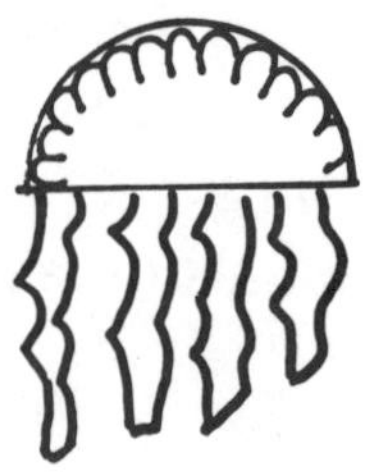

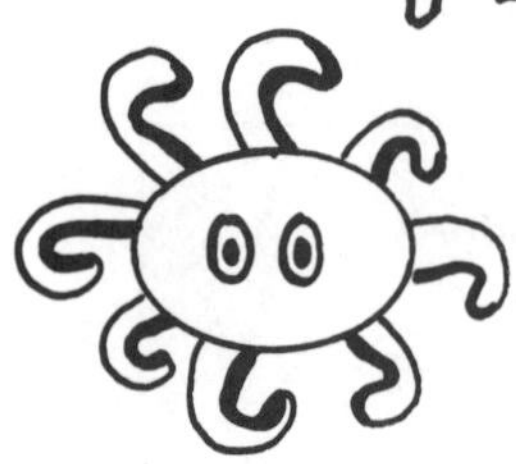

"Sole" Fish

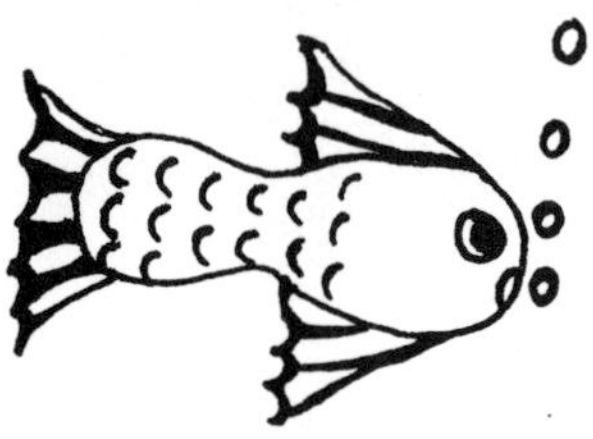

Materials

- construction paper
- felt-tipped markers or crayons
- glue, scissors
- scrap box

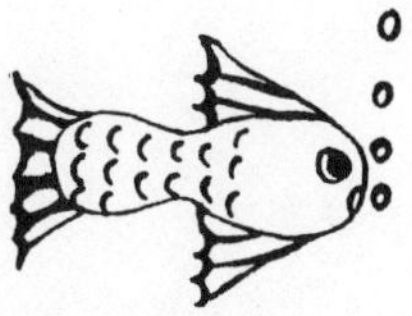

Directions

Trace around child's shoe on construction paper (any color). Have him cut it out and decorate, like a fish, with crayons, markers, and paper scraps.

Fish Bowl

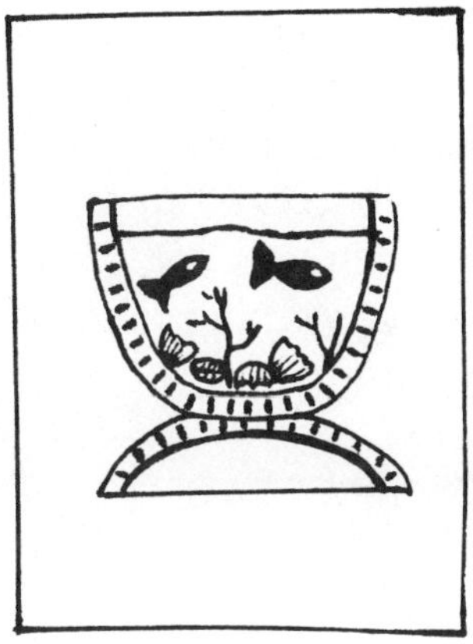

Materials

- 9" paper plate
- blue tempera paint
- brushes
- 3" squares of orange construction paper
- small shells and sand
- glue, scissors, pencils
- stapler

Directions

Day One— Cut a third of the paper plate off, saving the small piece to use as a base for the fish bowl. Paint the "water" part of the large piece blue (see illustration). Let dry.

Day Two— Attach base to blue bowl with staple. Glue sand and shells to bottom of bowl. Draw and cut fish shapes from orange squares. Glue above sand and shells.

Turtle Time

Concept

Shapes occur in nature.

Materials

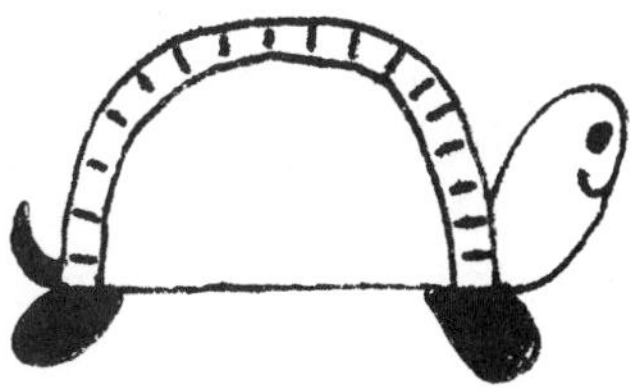

- 9" paper plate
- green tempera paint
- felt-tipped markers
- brushes, glue
- stapler

Directions

Day One —Paint paper plate green. Let dry.

Day Two —Cut paper plate in half. Use one half for turtle's body. Cut a head, two legs, and a tail from other half. Staple head to body. Glue on legs and tail. Add eyes and mouth with marker.

Red Crab

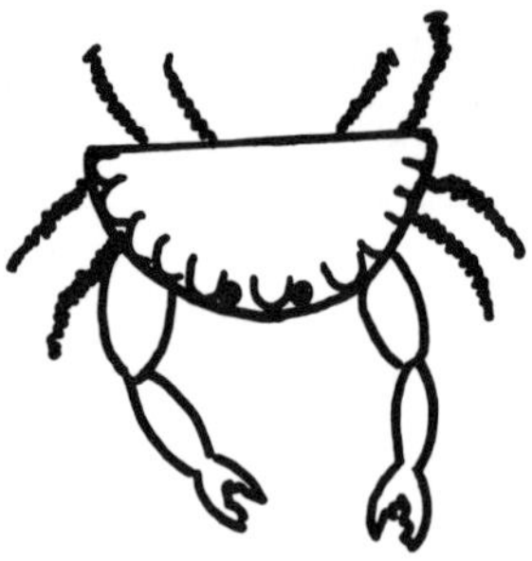

Materials

- half of 9" paper plate
- red tempera paint
- cardboard pattern for claw
- red construction paper
- eight 4" pieces of red pipe cleaners
- 2 buttons or black crumpled tissue (for eyes)
- glue, scissors, pencil, brush
- paper punch, string

Directions

Paint the paper plate half red on both sides. Let dry. Trace and cut out two claws from red paper. Glue to bottom of round side of plate. Push eight (four on each side) pipe cleaners through plate and bend to secure, forming feelers. Add eyes. Punch hole and tie string for hanging.

Vegetable Garden

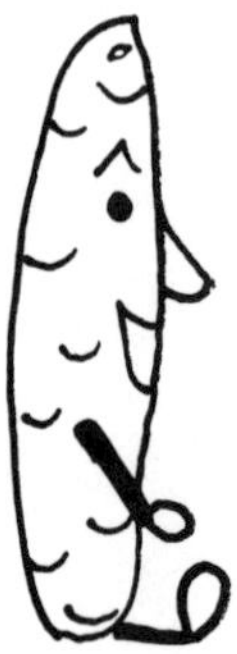

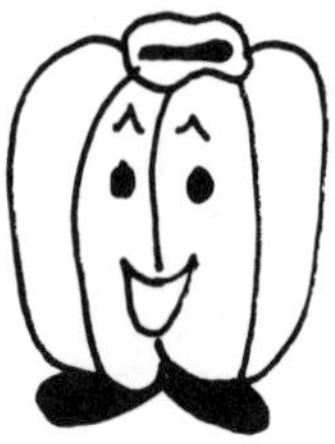

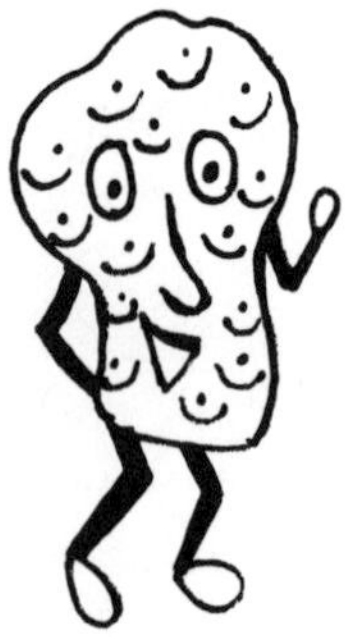

Concept

Vegetables can be identified by shape and color.

Materials

- 8" cardboard vegetable patterns
- 9" x 12" colored construction paper
- paper scrap box
- felt markers, pencils
- scissors, glue

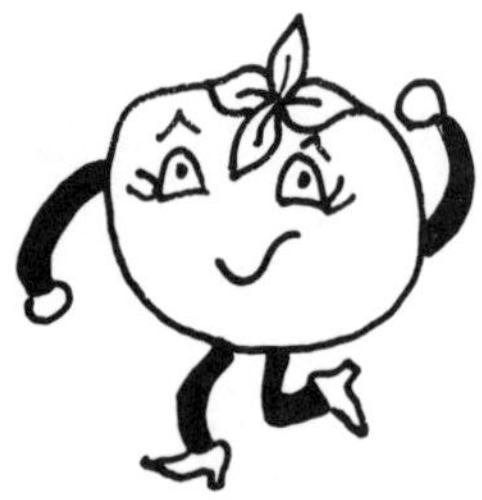

Directions

Have child choose a vegetable pattern to trace. After identifying this vegetable, let the child choose paper of an appropriate color. Trace and cut out shape. Add face with markers. Arms and legs may be cut from scraps and glued to shape.

June Bulletin Board Idea

Cover bulletin board with brown paper. Arrange "vegetables" on the board to make a class garden.

Little Ladybug

Motivation: Discuss the ladybug's colors and features—how the spots and antennae are used for protection.

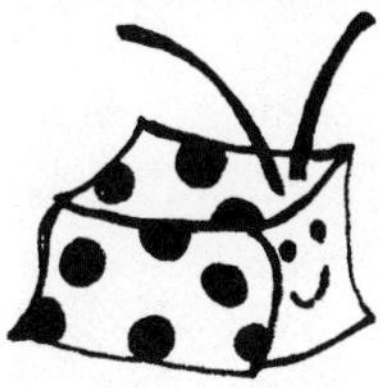

Materials

- one section of egg carton (not styrofoam)
- red tempera paint
- black felt-tipped marker
- two 3" pieces of pipe cleaner

Directions

Paint egg carton section red. Let dry. Use black marker for spots and eyes. Poke pipe cleaner antennae in body and curl ends slightly.

Parent Book

This project can be used for both Mother's Day and Father's Day. Simply change the appropriate words. The children are going to draw pictures as answers to a series of questions. These pictures will be assembled in a booklet to be given as a gift to Mom or Dad. This project may take several sessions, so begin early in May or June.

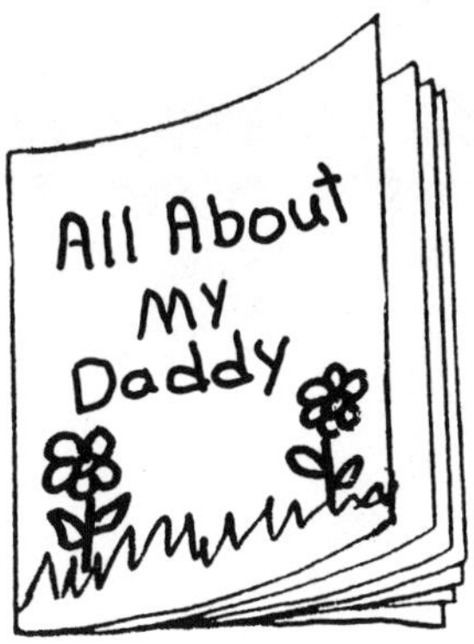

Directions

Print each of the questions below (or make up your own) on a separate ditto and duplicate for each child in the class. Have them *draw* the answer to each of the questions as it is read to them.

1. What does Daddy look like?
2. What is Daddy's favorite food?
3. What is Daddy's favorite color? Draw a flower with this color.
4. What do you and Daddy like to do together?
5. What does Daddy do while you are in school?

Other questions of your own may be added. Staple the pages together with a cover. Entitle the booklet *"All About My Daddy."*

Burlap Bookmark

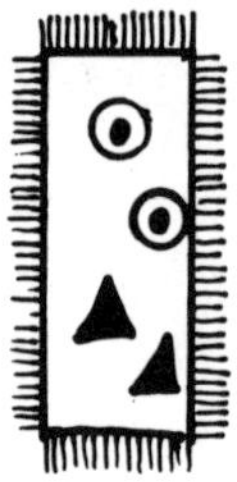

Materials

- 2 1/2" x 7" burlap strip (a light color would be best)
- tempera paint
- printing gadgets

Directions

Fringe all four sides of burlap strip. (Pull only about three or four strings per side to fringe.) Print with gadgets. Let dry. (Yarn tassels may be added at bottom using a slip knot.) Cards and wrapping paper for these gifts can also be printed at the same time.